# New Man...New World

Leighton Ford

A KEY-WORD BOOK
WORD BOOKS, Publisher
Waco, Texas

NEW MAN . . . NEW WORLD

A KEY WORD BOOK
Published by Pillar Books for Word Books, Publisher

Copyright © 1972 by Leighton Ford

First Key-Word Book edition—April 1976

Quotations from the Revised Standard Version of the Bible (RSV) copyright 1946, 1952, © 1971, 1973 by the Division of Christian Education of the National Council of the Churches of Christ in the United States of America, used by permission; *The New English Bible* (NEB) © The Delegates of The Oxford University Press and The Syndics of The Cambridge University Press, reprinted by permission; *The New Testament in Modern English* (Phillips), copyright © 1958, 1960, 1972 by J. B. Phillips, used by permission of the Macmillan Company; *The Living Bible, Paraphrased* (LB) copyright Tyndale House Publishers, 1971, used by permission; *The Holy Bible in Modern English, The Berkeley Version*, copyright 1945, 1958, Zondervan Publishing House; and *The Amplified Bible* (Amp), © 1965 by Zondervan Publishing House.

Library of Congress catalog card number: 72-88642
ISBN0-87680-873-9
Printed in the United States of America

*To Billy Graham
who inspired and encouraged me
to the work of an evangelist
and entrusted to me the privilege
of sharing God's good news on
the "Hour of Decision"*

# Preface

On my desk stands a sculpture of the "interrobang"—the newest punctuation mark which combines the question mark and the exclamation point.

It is certainly *the* mark of our day—an age which combines the most disturbing questions with the most exciting discoveries.

Religious discussion has moved in a few short years from Is God Dead? to Jesus Is Coming! And in this paradoxical time my purpose here is to reaffirm the age-old truth that in Christ new men create a new world!

We have been told to "do your own thing," to throw off the shackles of conformity, to express our personal freedom. There is a mania for change and a preoccupation with renewal—even revolution.

We are poised, it seems to me, at a strategic intersection of history. The Christian response dare not be passive. In the beginning the good news of Jesus Christ was a revolutionary force—a life-changing and history-shaping movement. A revival of that vigorous spirit must come!

In the conflicting forces of his time the Apostle Paul offered a revolutionary Christian life style: "Don't let the world around you squeeze you into its mold, but let God remold your minds from within."

It is my hope that in *New Man . . . New World* a pattern may emerge which will show a dynamic new life style in Christ as a genuine alternative to the confusion and despair around us.

Ideas for these messages came from many sources. I

must thank friends and authors who impressed them upon me, though I cannot remember all their names.

A few brief words cannot adequately express my gratitude to my wife, Jeanie, whose unfailing love, trust, and counsel have helped to keep my mind and heart fresh; to my energetic and cheerful secretary, Leola Linkous, who always does a superb job on the typing, and to Floyd Thatcher of Word who persuaded me that the chapters in this book, originally given as sermons on the "Hour of Decision," could be a further inspiration in this new form.

LEIGHTON FORD

# Contents

# New Man...New World

# 1

# Identity Crisis

MODERN MAN IS SUFFERING from a kind of spiritual amnesia. He is passing through a deep crisis of identity.

Many businessmen are torn between the nearly total demands of the company and the needs of their family. Housewives devour popular articles on the "feminine mystique" and try to figure out whether it's enough to be "just a housewife" or whether they need a career, too, in order to be fulfilled. Students march in picket lines with the sign, "I am a human being; do not bend, fold, spindle, or mutilate." And teenagers drop out of the conformity cult, let their hair grow, take off their shoes, and put on beads as if to say, "Look, just because my hair is long, am I no longer a man, a human being? Is a person just a haircut on a clotheshorse?"

One of the TV networks produced a special called "In Search of a Past." It was part of a series on black America, and it centered on the search of the young Negro to find his identity. Since many Afro-Americans believe that the black man can only find self-respect through recovering the lost heritage of the past African culture, several young Negroes were taken to West Africa for a month by the network. They mingled with the people, talked with students their own age, saw the way Africans live in the new modern cities and in the bush country, and at the end of the month they were asked what they had found.

Their reactions were mixed. Some were disappointed because modern Africa was so much like modern America, complete with transistors, Cokes, and guitars. Others decided that black Americans really had more in common with white Americans than they did with Africans. And some were excited at discovering their roots from the past. But the impression was strong that it was going to take a lot more than a jet ride across the Atlantic to recover a lost identity.

The original American astronauts were given a battery of psychological tests. One test was this, "Give twenty answers to the question, 'Who am I?' "

Try to answer that. You'll find it's an interesting exercise. I am a human being, a male, a son, a husband and a father, a friend, a Canadian citizen, an American resident. I am a taxpayer, a tennis enthusiast, a communicator of the gospel, a reader of newspapers and books, a car driver, et cetera.

Now when you have made your list and have run out of things to add, have you really answered the question? Do you really know who you are?

Hermann Hesse, the German novelist, said, "The true profession of a man is to find his way to himself. I have become a writer, but I have not become a human being."

Because we are searching for identity, we tend to become imitators of other people, like a little boy mimicking his favorite baseball player—wearing his hat and waving his bat just like Johnny Bench does. We paste on bits and pieces of other people. We make love like some actor. We play golf like Gary Player. Now, part of this process is natural because we learn by imitating others. But the tragedy comes when we never find our true self. As someone said, "We begin life as an original, and we end up as a copy."

So where do we go next? If going back to Africa or Ireland doesn't do it, if our family relationships with our parents are all fouled up, if science can tell us what an atom is but not what a man is, where do we turn?

Perhaps it is time to turn to our Bible and see if it has something to say to this dilemma of modern man. One of the key ideas that runs through it is the idea of the image of God. In Genesis we read, "God said, Let us make man in our image, after our likeness: and let them have dominion . . . So God created man in his own image, in the image of God created he him; male and female created he them" (1:26, 27). Genesis 5:1 (Amp.) tells us that "When God created man He made him in the likeness of God."

Notice in these two passages that the sacredness of

sex and the sacredness of human life both hang on "the image of God." And I believe that part of the reason for the sexual promiscuity that we see today is a perverted drive to find this relationship with God for which we were made.

Now, this idea of the image of God is carried over into the New Testament. First Corinthians 11:7 says that man "is the image and glory of God." James 3:9 (RSV) speaks of the sin of cursing "men, who are made in the likeness of God."

What does the Bible mean when it says that men are made in God's image? Well, first of all, it doesn't mean that we bear the physical likeness of God, because "God is a Spirit" (John 4:24). God doesn't have a human body. It means that spiritually we are made *for* God. Man is not God; man is dependent on God. But man is more than an animal, more than muscles and flesh and bone. Man is also a spirit—with a mind, intelligence, a moral sense of right and wrong—and this is what gives him a capacity to have a relationship with God.

On one occasion Jesus asked to see a coin that was used to pay taxes. "Whose likeness is this?" He demanded. And they said, "Caesar's" (cf. Luke 20:24). It is interesting to know that the word Jesus used is *eikon*, "likeness," the same word that is used of man made in the likeness of God (1 Cor. 11:7). The coin was not Caesar, but it belonged to him because his image was stamped on it. So man is not God, but he belongs to God because man's nature has been stamped with God's likeness.

You see, if you want to find your identity, you have to go back—not back to your childhood, not back to your homeland across the seas—but to Eden, back to God.

The Bible tells us something else. Men bear this image of God, but it has been shattered and defaced because of sin. Man has rebelled against the status given him. Man didn't want to be God's image; he wanted to be God! "Ye shall be as gods" (Gen. 3:5) was the temptation that came to Adam and Eve. This is what sin fundamentally is—"God-Almightiness," the big "I," the superman, turning from God to our own way.

Once upon a time, in the beginning, man reflected the beauty and goodness of God as clearly as still water in a pool reflects the shining moon from its surface on a summer night. But the chilling winds of our rebellion have churned the water into waves. The moon still shines, but the pool no longer reflects it from broken surface. And the true Light is no longer reflected from our broken, disordered lives. The identity crisis is a squalling, terrified baby born from the womb of man's first sin.

The Scripture says this broken image of God shines again in Jesus Christ (2 Cor. 4:4). He is "the image of the invisible God" (Col. 1:15). Jesus Christ is the picture of what God is like because He is God the Son. He is also the image of what true man, genuine man, authentic humanity, is like.

We are living today in what has been called the age of the anti-hero. Yet we desperately need heroes—models of what it means to be alive, what it means to be good, what it means to be committed, what it means to be a man! Where can we find them?

Some months ago the students at Harvard University were going through a craze for old Humphrey Bogart movies. *Time* magazine said that this was part of the student "identity crisis." Bogart was a character with whom they could identify.

*Parade* magazine took a poll of twenty-one hundred young people sixteen to twenty-three years of age. They asked, "Is there any living . . . figure whom you admire or respect or with whom you identify?" Over 53 percent said no.

Well, I would like to suggest that in the Person of Jesus Christ is One in whom you can find your identity, whether you are under thirty or over thirty. A girl at Baylor University said, "I studied Jesus Christ not just to learn who He was but to know who I am."

Bishop Stephen Neill points out, "Before (the lost image of God in man) can be restored, the true human reality into which man is to be transformed must be visibly set forth before his eyes. This it was that was accomplished in the life and death of Jesus of Nazareth."

You may be surprised if you get a Bible and start to read about Jesus Christ, how in Him you will see the true pattern for your own life. This happens to me frequently. Sometimes I get the feeling that I have goals that I can accomplish by my own efforts. Then I read about Jesus kneeling in prayer, and I realize that if Jesus, being the Son of God, the real Man, needed to pray, how much more I do! I am not sufficient without God. Or sometimes as a preacher I get all lost in words and ideas and concepts. Then I look at Jesus, and what do I see? Jesus was involved with people. He didn't just preach about leprosy; He touched a leper. He didn't just lecture on hunger; He fed people with empty stomachs.

And then there is something even more wonderful that the Bible tells us about this image of God. You see, if this were just a great ideal that I saw in Jesus, I couldn't identify with Him. "Be like Jesus!" Who? Me?

Yes, me . . . and you. The Bible tells us that Jesus Christ can actually share Himself with us and give us a new identity. God's purpose is to conform us "to the image of his Son" (Rom. 8:29). That is why He sent Jesus into the world. Jesus didn't come just to live out a great ideal. He came to die and to come alive. He died to pour out His life and put it in the believer. That is why we are not just supposed to admire Jesus. We are to put Him on (Rom. 13:14)! "Put on the new nature, created after the likeness of God in true righteousness and holiness' " (Eph. 4:24, RSV).

You see, the likeness to God that we had at the first, the likeness that we lost by sin, is created again in us when our lives are joined to Christ.

Paul the Apostle often called himself "a man in Christ" (2 Cor. 12:2). That is true identity—to be in Christ, to know that He has received me into His own life, to know that He has started on a lifelong project of making me like Him, and that someday I "shall also bear the image of the man of heaven" (1 Cor. 15:49, RSV).

That is Christian identity. I know my past and where I came from. I came from God. I know what went wrong; I tried to play God instead of being satisfied to be a real man. I know my future; my destiny is Christ. And I know the present; I can face myself now—my problems, my hang-ups, my assets, my faults—because I have turned myself over to God. And He has accepted me as I am because Jesus Christ died for me, and He is working in everything that happens to help me discover who I am to God! And here is a paradox. As I become more and more by God's power like Jesus Christ, I don't become less like Leighton Ford. Only as I become like Christ can I be what Leighton Ford was meant to be.

Bob Slocum, an aerospace engineer with NASA, wrote, "I became convinced that Jesus Christ is the God behind the physical universe. The important question then became not whether I thought God was real, but whether God thought I was real. The idea took hold that in Christ God does love me and takes me seriously; and I began the experiment of placing my life in His hands and setting out to discover what it means to live for Him."

There are three "you's"—the person you think you are, the person others think you are, and the person God knows you are and can be through Christ. Will the real *you* please stand up and find your identity in Christ?

# 2

# Soul Power

A FEW YEARS AGO a lonely, eccentric miner disappeared in the state of Arizona. He left behind an estate valued at $200,000. After he was declared legally dead, they found a handwritten will stipulating that the money he left should be used to provide "research on some scientific proof of a soul in a human body which leaves at death." Scores of organizations and individuals who thought they could prove this claimed the money, and a judge was asked to rule on whether man indeed had a soul. The last I read, the estate was awarded to the American Society for Psychical Research.

For many years now the soul seems to have been the forgotten man. Unbelieving educators and psychologists and sociologists have drummed into the minds of the public that man's soul can be explained away, that man's mind and man's personality can be accounted for simply as electro-chemical discharges in the brain.

This materialistic doctrine has been a poison in the bloodstream of society. To no small degree the denial of man's spiritual reality must be held accountable for the senseless violence, the mindless brutality, the degradation of sex, the moral apathy, the "eat, drink, and be merry" philosophy, and the lack of purpose which more and more characterizes the lives of men today. This is what really should be concerning us, not the financial devaluation of gold or the dollar but the spiritual devaluation of man!

Some time ago Billy Graham talked with one of the entertainment industry's top comedy writers. This man said that the kookiest person he had ever met was a man who went around buying up people's souls for twenty-five cents. He did this to show that people really gave very little value to their souls. In the office in which he worked he had been successful in buying over half the souls!

I believe that the question we need to hear today is the one Jesus Christ asked two thousand years ago, "What shall it profit a man, if he shall gain the whole world, and lose his own soul?" (Mark 8:36).

I also believe that you cannot keep spiritual reality down. The truth of what man really is keeps coming back to us. And it is interesting to note that the very word *soul* has come back into our vocabulary. The black community in America has popularized terms such as "soul brother," "soul music," "soul food," and "soul culture." People are groping after the things of the spirit, and yet very few people understand what man's soul is. Ray Charles, the singer, was asked what "soul" is, and he said, "It's like electricity—we don't really know what it is. But it's a force that can light a room."

Now the word *soul* as Jesus used it actually should be translated "life." "What shall it profit a man, if he shall gain the whole world, and lose his own life?" Or as it is put in Luke's Gospel, "For what does it profit a man if he gains the whole world and loses or forfeits himself?" (9:25, RSV).

When most people think of the soul, they think of some vague little round spiritual object imprisoned someplace in the body. But that is not the way the Bible speaks of it. In the Bible the soul is man's life. It is man's real self. It is the thing that makes you *you!* Your soul is the breath of your life. It is the seat of your emotions. It is the part of you that loves and hates and grieves and desires and feels. It is your behavior mechanism, the part of you that wills and decides.

In other words, the soul is man's total self. It is man's individuality. It is what distinguishes you from every other human being. In your soul lies your self, your ego, your personality. It isn't really right to say that you *have* a soul. What we should say is that you *are* a soul.

Now, did you know that animals also are souls? Genesis 2:7 tells us that at the creation God "breathed into (man's) nostrils the breath of life; and man became a living soul." But that identical word, "living soul," or "living creature," is also used in the same chapter to speak of birds and fish and animals. They have

23

souls, too—behavior mechanisms, the ability to think and feel and act.

But there is one huge difference. God has protected animals by directing their souls and their behavior through instinct. Take the salmon for example. The salmon has a guidance system which automatically tells it when it is time to leave the ocean to go back up river to spawn. Birds have an instinct that tells them it is time to head south for the winter and north for the summertime. But man is different. Man's soul isn't run by instinct, by an automatic guidance system.

God could have made us like that. He could have made you like a salmon so that you had to follow His program. But this would not have been pleasing to God. If we were that way, we wouldn't be real people. You see, an animal may follow God's plan unconsciously. But God made you and me so that He Himself could live in the soul, so that we could obey Him because we wanted to, and so that He could control our souls by faith and love and obedience.

This is our glory—that we can meet God personally, that we can answer when He speaks through His Word and by His Holy Spirit. We are made for God. We are made for greatness. We are made for a rendezvous with destiny in this life and the life to come. We are more than a human refrigerator. We have instincts; we need food and water and shelter. We have a desire for sex, but we have a hunger for God that food and water and shelter and sex can never satisfy. There is a place in our souls that only God can ever fill.

I know that there are those who reduce men to the level of animals. There are computer scientists who insist that man is merely an early-model computer. Bertrand Russell wrote in *A Free Man's Worship* that man is simply "the outcome of accidental collocations of atoms."

But that leads me to ask, if you go along with that, then why do you act as if man mattered? Do you love anybody? Why? Do you respect anybody? Why?

Do you trust anybody? Why? Do you believe in man's right to dignity and freedom? If so, why? You see, if man is just an animal or a machine, then why not manipulate him like an animal or a machine?

A friend of mine was in Paris during the student riots a few years ago at the Sorbonne. He got into a conversation with a tall bearded man who turned out to be an airline pilot. "What are you doing down here?" asked my friend.

"I'm protesting this rotten, lousy world."

"Do you believe in God?" asked my friend.

"No, I'm an atheist."

Then my friend asked him, "Do you love anybody?"

The bearded man thought a moment, and then lowered his eyes and said, "Yes, I love a woman, not my wife, a woman by whom I have had a child; and she is dying of leukemia."

"But why do you love her? Why don't you forget her? She's just a worthless thing." At this, the big man started to hit him, but my friend quietly added, "Wait a minute. On your principles she is just a collection of chemicals. What makes her worth loving?" And he said that pilot walked off thoughtfully, carrying a copy of the Gospel of John which he promised to read.

I hope he did read it because the only place in all the world where we can find a reason to love and value people is in the Bible, in God's revelation that man is not an animal, not a machine, but a living soul created by an infinite, personal Creator in His very own image.

Jesus asked, "What shall it profit a man, if he gain the whole world, and lose his soul—his life, his self?" The answer is a big, fat zero! The profit is nothing! The loss is everything! So you make your fortune, so you win the championship, so your name goes up in the headlines, so you can afford to buy the house you want, so you wear the right clothes and you are accepted in the right set—so what? If you lose your real self, if you end up with a God-shaped blank in your soul, if you have an eternal hunger that nothing can satisfy, what's the profit?

That's why Jesus warned over and over again, "Beware, watch out—you're in danger of losing your soul!" He warned in Mark 8:35 (RSV), "Whoever would save his life"—save his soul—"will lose it." Now, you can say no to God. You can decide to run your life your way instead of God's way. But if you do, you don't find yourself; you lose yourself. "He who loves his life loses it," said Jesus (John 12:25, RSV).

On another occasion Jesus warned His followers, "Do not fear those who kill the body but cannot kill the soul; rather fear him who can destroy both soul and body in hell" (Matt. 10:28, RSV). You can lose your soul in this life and in the life to come because when sin cuts you off from God, your soul survives, but it survives only in a kind of living death.

In our world today there are millions of people who are successful in the eyes of other people, but they have lost themselves. They live with a terrible feeling of emptiness, a sense of loneliness, a burden of guilt, and a fear of death. Perhaps you are one of those people. You are reaching out for something, but you don't know what. You are trying to find the answer in drugs or in sex or in power or in art or in alcohol or in business activity, and all of the time your soul is really crying out, "O God, I seek *Thee*. My soul is thirsting for *Thee*."

Jesus Christ asked two questions about the soul. He asked, "What shall it profit a man, if he shall gain the whole world, and lose his own soul?" And the answer to that is, "Nothing." But He asked another question, "What shall a man give in exchange for his soul?" (Mark 8:37).

Notice what He said—not, "What shall a man *take* for his soul?" You and I know how cheaply men will sell their souls—a few drinks, a passing affair, the momentary popularity of the crowd. But Jesus didn't ask here what a man would *take* for his soul. He said, "What

26

will a man *give* for his soul?" Once you have sold your soul, once you have lost it, once you have scarred it, what can you give to get it back? And the answer to that, too, is "Nothing." No man can buy his soul back.

The only one who can answer that question is the One who asked it, the Lord Jesus Christ. And He did answer it one day when He said, "The Son of man . . . came . . . to give his life"—his soul—"as a ransom for many" (Mark 10:45, RSV). Tears can't buy a soul back; remorse can't buy it back; good resolutions and repentance can't even buy back a soul. Only the blood of the Son of man Himself shed for the forgiveness of our sins (Matt. 26:28) can cleanse and restore your soul. That awful, terrible, bloody, agonizing death of Jesus on the Cross is God's price tag on your soul.

I remember an Australian preacher who told me that a streetwalker once approached him in London and tried to sell herself to him. Instead of brushing her away he said, "How much? What's your price?"

She named a figure.

"Oh," he said, "that's not enough."

"Not enough!" she said. "What do you mean?" She thought he was poking fun at her.

But then he went on to say, "You deserve more than that. Jesus Christ died for you. That's how much you're worth. And you're selling yourself too cheaply." That conversation eventually was the means of leading that girl to Jesus Christ.

And today that same Christ wants to bring every man back to Himself. He'll restore dignity and freedom and eternal life to the soul. He is anxious to give every person real "soul power."

# 3

# Do His Thing

WHILE DRIVING DOWN THE STREET one day, I heard a radio ad for a life insurance company. They were selling a new policy which they called, "Total Way of Life." The commercial went something like this, "Our policy is tailored to fit into your total way of life. It allows *you* to make decisions. *You* choose, *you* select what you want out of life. A college education for your kids? A comfortable house in the right neighborhood? Carefree retirement years? You make the decision, and we'll tailor our policy to your total way of life."

It struck me that this slogan fits the mind-set, the mood, of our day. It's like the popular phrase, "Do your own thing." After all, it's your life. Don't let anybody else tell you how to run it. You make the decisions. You call the shots.

In one sense this is all good because each of us is an individual. You've got certain God-given rights and gifts. You can't fit into somebody else's mold. You've got to become what you are.

But at another level this "do-your-own-thing" mind-set has something almost sinister to it. It has become a symbol of the revolt against authority. And our society is being ripped apart today by the tension between anarchy on the one hand and authoritarianism on the other.

"Anarchy" simply means to be without a ruler. It means to be without any order, any authority, or any ruling power. And it's nothing new. In the days of the Judges the Bible says, ". . . there was no king in Israel; every man did what was right in his own eyes" (Judg. 17:6, RSV). That was anarchy.

Today, anarchy has become a total way of life for some people. Can you picture a hippie sitting cross-legged in his pad, wearing his beads and smoking his pot. He has dropped out of what he regards as straight society and is trying to do his own thing. He has rejected all the things he thinks society is trying to impose on him. He's a kind of gentle, mild-mannered anarchist.

And on the other extreme you have the yippies, the

militant anarchists. The radical left among the students actually wants to do away with all government, all structure, and all authority.

Some time ago British pop singer, Mick Jagger, a member of the Rolling Stones, was arrested for possessing drugs illegally. At his trial he said, "It's when authority won't allow something that I dig in. I'm against anything that interferes with individual freedom. As a nonconformist I won't accept what other people say is right. And there are hundreds like me, thousands."

Now the hippies and the yippies are just the dramatic fringes of an anarchy which pervades every area of life. Sometimes it seems that everything that has been nailed down is coming loose. One observer says, " 'Authority' on college and university campuses is virtually a swear word."

In the home many parents are afraid to say no to their children. Students are protesting that college and university authorities have no right to make rules as to whether a young man may have a girl in his room. The most authoritarian religious groups are finding that control over their followers is coming unglued.

Now, questioning authority is not new. And we can't say that it is absolutely bad, because to some extent it is part of growing up. Did you know that the very word *exist* actually means "to stand out from"? The young person who is trying to find out who he is, to be himself, has to stand out from others, to question authority to some extent, and even sometimes to buck authority when it's wrong. And I believe that within limits God has set things up so change can come about in this way.

But today there are two factors which, as David Hubbard, president of Fuller Theological Seminary, points out, make the revolt against authoritarianism so intense. *One* is the rapid rate of change. Everything is changing so quickly. Our information goes out of date so rapidly. And it is fantastically difficult for any-

31

body or any institution—the home or the school or the government or the church—to keep up with the changes. And then the *second* factor that intensifies the questioning of authority is the high price tag we place on personal freedom. We want the individual to have the right to his own beliefs and his own opinions.

What does this mean? Obviously, a rigid authoritarianism, trying to stuff convictions down the throat of somebody else, is out. But that still leaves us with the problem of true authority. You see, ultimately you've got to have some authority to follow. It may be yourself; it may be somebody else. What is your authority? Do you have an authority? Whom do you believe? Who has the last word in your life?

For example, do you believe that people are important? Do you believe that we ought to respect the rights and beliefs of others? Why do you believe that? Where did we ever get the idea that we should care about individuals and that people matter?

It came from the Bible—the story that God made man, that God loves man, and that the Son of God laid down his life for man. Never forget that the great drive for freedom today in Africa and Asia and throughout the world wasn't started by the emissaries of communism singing the songs of Karl Marx but by the missionaries who came singing the freedom song of Christ.

This leads me to believe that if we want to know about true authority and true freedom, we need to look at what the Bible has to say about it. First of all, the Bible teaches that *the final Authority is God*. His authority is complete and eternal and unchanging. "I am the Lord, I change not" (Mal. 3:6). "The earth is the Lord's and the fulness thereof" (Ps. 24:1). "Of him, and through him, and to him, are all things" (Rom. 11:36). These are the statements of Scripture. And we will never know what true authority is until we have recognized the authority of God.

At the bottom, sin is spiritual anarchy. Sin is rebel-

32

lion against the authority of God. Turn back to the early pages of the Bible and you will find that when the devil tempted Eve, his temptation was to doubt God's authority. He said, "Did God say, 'You shall not eat of any tree of the garden'?" (Gen. 3:1, RSV). "God is not the Authority," he said, "you are. Don't listen to God." And then the psalmist spoke of the revolt of the world's leaders against God: "The kings of the earth . . . take counsel together, against the Lord and his anointed, saying, 'Let us burst their bonds asunder, and cast their cords from us' " (Ps. 2:2, RSV).

At its root the anarchy of our day is a symptom of the spirit of lawlessness, the refusal of men to recognize the authority of God and of His Word in their lives.

The biggest question we have to settle is this: Did I get here by chance or did I get here by God's design? Because, you see, if I am here by chance, then I am the ultimate authority, I am my own man, and I can call the shots as I see them. But if I'm here by God's design, then God is the ultimate authority; I am God's man, and God is the One who calls the shots in my life. He won't force me to go His way. He'll even allow me to say no. But even the right to choose hell finally comes from God's authority.

And then the Bible says that *God has placed authority in His Word*. "For ever, O Lord, thy word is settled in heaven" (Ps. 119:89). And Jesus said, "Heaven and earth shall pass away, but My words shall never pass away" (Matt. 24:35, Berkeley).

The Bible also teaches that *God has delegated certain authority to men*. God has delegated to governments authority to rule and to restrain evil. In Romans 13:1 Paul says, "Let every person be subject to the governing authorities. For there is no authority except from God, and those that exist have been instituted by God" (RSV). Now of course, no man, no ruler, is perfect. And the demands of a ruler may sometimes be evil and contradict the commands of God. That is

33

when "We must obey God rather than men" (Acts 5:29, RSV).

In addition, God has established the home, and in the home He has given authority to parents to bring up their children "in the discipline and instruction of the Lord" (Eph. 6:4, RSV). That is why the Bible commands, "Children, obey your parents in the Lord, for this is right" (v. 1). Notice the qualification: obey them "in the Lord." It is our duty to submit to authority in every area of life, *unless* that authority goes against the will of God. And I believe a major reason for the breakdown of authority today is that many parents have abdicated their authority in the home. We have sown anarchy in our homes, and we have reaped anarchy in society.

Again, the Bible teaches that *God has placed His authority uniquely in the hands of Jesus Christ.* Jesus said, "All authority in heaven and on earth has been given to me" (Matt. 28:8, RSV).

His teaching was with authority. When He finished the Sermon on the Mount, it says the people "were astonished at his teaching, for he taught them as one who had authority, and not as their scribes" (Matt. 7:28, 29, RSV). With authority He called men. He said, "Follow me," "Come after me," "If any man will come after me, let him deny himself, and take up his cross, and follow me" (Matt. 16:24). He demanded first place, to be the Authority, in the lives of His followers.

And then Jesus Christ forgave sins with authority. On one occasion when they brought a sick man to Him, Jesus said, "Son, your sins are forgiven." When those who heard accused Him of blasphemy, Jesus answered, "I will show you that I have authority to forgive sins." And to demonstrate it, He healed the paralyzed man and made him walk again (Matt. 9:2–7, RSV).

Jesus also said that some day with authority He would judge men. John 5:26, 27 (RSV), "The Father . . . has granted the Son . . . authority to execute judgment, because he is the Son of man." And at the end of the Sermon on the Mount, Jesus pictures Himself as the One who at the last days will have authority to settle the eternal destiny of men.

Now you know, there is a strange paradox about Jesus Christ. When He taught about Himself, He was so utterly self-centered. He said, "I am the final Authority." And yet in the way He acted, He was so selfless. He claimed to be the Son of God, yet He played with children. He claimed to be the King of heaven, and yet He was always thinking about how He could help other people. He claimed to be the final Judge of men, and yet He offered Himself to die on a Cross to be their Savior. Jesus didn't impose Himself. He wanted to win men by love and by what He did on that Cross.

Recently a friend of mine was giving a series of talks at a university. In the barber shop he met a young mathematics teacher. They got into a discussion about the Christian faith, and my friend explained that if he committed his life to Christ, he'd have to move over and let Christ take the center. This young teacher thought a moment and then blurted out, "I'm very reluctant for this decentralization."

That is a magnificent, up-to-date term for conversion—"decentralization." Nothing less than this is meant when a person becomes a Christian and lives as a Christian. It means a total way of life in which you move over and say, "Jesus Christ, take control of the center of my life."

He isn't a static Christ. He doesn't ask us to tie ourselves to the history of a hundred years ago. He is changing the world by His gospel into a world of love and justice, and He wants to enlist each one of us in His cause.

Remember, too, that He is not an authoritarian Christ, though He has all authority. He will not force anybody to follow Him. He let the rich young ruler reject Him (Mark 10:22); and He will not stop us from

35

choosing that broad way that leads to destruction (Matt. 7:13). He will not impose Himself on our thinking. But if we turn control of our lives over to Him, we will find true freedom in His authority.

# 4

# Why Doesn't God Hear?

At ONE TIME Yungay was a village high in the Andes Mountains of Peru. Today Yungay is no more. It is buried under a sea of mud—totally wiped out by the terrible earthquake which shook Peru and left over 35,000 people dead or missing.

In a vivid firsthand report from Yungay at the time of the disaster, journalist Lamberto Guzman reported, "We were praying and terrified when we heard the infernal rumbling of the mass of mud and rocks falling from the Andes. All of us ran to higher ground, all of us who could. The injured who remained were swept away. The earthquake lasted three minutes and forty seconds. Men and women were holding hands in groups, shouting to God to have compassion. God didn't hear us. The earth kept trembling."

"God didn't hear us." Those four stark words confront us with the problem of evil. Why does a good, strong loving God permit pain, suffering, and evil in this world? Why are babies born blind? Why do good people suffer? Why do bad people seem to be successful? Why doesn't God stop it all?

If God is all-powerful, then He can't be good and loving or else He would stop all this suffering. Or if God is really loving and good, then He can't be all-powerful. He must not be able to stamp out evil.

Is there any way out of this dilemma?

Let's acknowledge right away there are no glib and easy answers to this profound question. For thousands of years ordinary people and great thinkers have wrestled with this question of evil. The earliest book in the Bible, the Book of Job, deals with the question of why a good man suffers. Jesus Himself on the Cross said, "My God, why . . . ?" (Mark 15:34). Apparently God has not seen fit to disclose the full answer. Deuteronomy 29:29 says, "The secret things belong unto the Lord our God," and the mystery of iniquity and evil is one of them.

"Well," says the skeptic, "why don't you just admit

there's no answer because there's no God to give an answer? If there's no God, then you don't have to explain evil. It's just part of a senseless world."

Yes, but if there is no God, then a greater question emerges—the problem of good. How have we come to think there's a difference between good and evil? Where did the idea of "good" come from? You see, bad means nothing unless you have good to contrast with it. Why do we say that courage is good and cowardice is bad? Why do we say that kindness is good and selfishness is bad? You see, evil is a problem to us just because God has given us a moral sense of right and wrong.

The Bible does not give us the final and complete answer as to where evil comes from, but it does give us some important clues. It tells us, for example, in Genesis 1:31 that God made man good, "God saw everything that he had made, and, behold, it was very good." Man was not created evil. God made us for an unending life of fellowship with Himself.

The Bible also indicates that God gave man the capacity to obey or to disobey Him. If man had obeyed God, there would have been no problem. But man tried to become God. Man rebelled. As Romans 5:12 says, "Wherefore, by one man sin entered into the world, and death by sin; and so death passed upon all men, for that all have sinned." It is man who is responsible for sin, not God. And much of the suffering in our world can be traced directly to the evil choices that men make. We can't blame God for drunken driving. We can't blame God for the man who makes a crooked decision in government. We can't blame God for the dishonest businessman. We can't blame God for those who pollute our natural resources. We can't blame God for cheating and lying and selfishness or for negligence in construction when a building falls down. Man is to blame for these.

"Well," someone says, "why didn't God make man so he couldn't sin?"

39

He could have. But then man would have been a machine; we would have been robots, not men.

I remember a student at a university meeting who once asked me, "Mr. Ford, if God knew that men would sin, why did He go ahead and make us and give us the power to choose?"

I thought a moment and then answered, "Apparently God thought *you* were worth the risk."

The Scripture also tells us that it is God's mercy that keeps Him from wiping out all evil. Lamentations 3: 22 says, "It is of the Lord's mercies that we are not consumed, because his compassions fail not." If God chose, He could wipe out evil right now. A time is coming when He will. The devil and all his evil works will be judged. Meanwhile God's mercy prevails. Suppose that God decided to wipe out all evil at midnight tonight. If He did, He would certainly do a thorough job. How many of us would be left at 1 A.M.? It's God's mercy that gives us a chance to repent.

Now the Scripture also tells us that God has an enemy. Man is not alone in the world. God's Word tells us of an enemy named Satan. He appears in various forms. God allows Satan limited powers. He allowed Satan to cause Job to suffer (Job 1:12). Jesus told a story of the wheat and the tares in which a farmer's harvest was ruined. And He explained it, "An enemy has done this" (Matt. 13:28, RSV). You see, the devil finds pleasure in ruining God's creation and causing misery. And Satan accounts for some of the disease and suffering in the world.

In the story of *Robinson Crusoe,* Man Friday asks, "If God is so much stronger than the devil, why doesn't God kill the devil?"

Robinson Crusoe answered, "You may as well ask why God does not kill you and me when we do wicked things."

According to the Scriptures, God permits some suffering as judgment. Galatians 6:7 says, "Whatsoever a man soweth, that shall he also reap." Sin brings death. Miriam, Moses' sister, was struck with leprosy because of her sin (Num. 12:1–10). Ananias and Sapphira in the New Testament were struck dead because they lied to God (Acts 5:1–10).

But the Scripture also indicates that not all suffering is a punishment for sin. When Jesus was asked one day whether a blind man or his parents had sinned and caused his blindness, He answered, "Neither . . . he was born blind that the works of God should be made manifest in him" (cf. John 9:3). When Job suffered, his friends decided that he must have sinned some terrible sin for all of the calamities to befall him, but it was not so.

It seems clear from the examples in the Bible that whenever someone does suffer because of his misdeeds, he is never left in doubt as to the fact that it is sin that is being punished.

Now God allows some suffering because there are some things to be accomplished in our character that can only be brought about by suffering and trial. First Peter 1:7 (NEB) teaches, "Even gold passes through the assayer's fire, and more precious than . . . gold is faith which has stood the test. These trials come so that your faith may prove itself worthy of all praise, glory, and honour when Jesus Christ is revealed."

As a young doctor who was going through great suffering said, "I have learned that God is more concerned with my character than with my comfort." Great civilizations and great people are made not in softness but in challenge and in response to that challenge. Augustine once said, "God had one Son without sin; he has no sons without suffering."

It is very possible that you are going through some great time of trial. You wonder if you can stand the pressure. You feel like crying out and saying, "God, stop it!" But remember that just as diamonds are formed from carbon under the tremendous pressure of

41

tons of earth, so God is allowing character to be formed under the pressure of your circumstances.

The most important thing the Bible teaches is that God feels and shares our suffering. There are many questions the Bible doesn't answer about suffering. I can't explain today why God would allow thousands to perish in an earthquake. But even if we had all the intellectual answers, would it help us much to have them if that's all we had, even when what we really need is a practical answer as to how to meet suffering? The Bible tells us that God has come to be with us in the pain and the sorrow and the sin and the suffering. He is a God who is "touched with the feeling of our infirmities" (Heb. 4:15).

God is the great Sufferer. Can you believe that? That's why He came in Jesus Christ, who was "a man of sorrows, and acquainted with grief" (Isa. 53:3).

And God has fully met the problem of evil in the gift and the sacrifice of His Son. That is why ultimately the Cross where Jesus Christ died is the answer to the problem of evil. Men have tried to answer this question of evil by denying certain things. Some deny that evil is real. Some deny that God is good. Some deny that God is powerful and sovereign. But the Cross of Jesus answers evil by affirming all three of these things.

The Cross tells us that evil and sin are real. The crucifixion of Jesus Christ was the most flagrant crime of all history. Sin is a terrible reality, says the Cross. And we are personally responsible, says the Cross. As the old Negro spiritual puts it, *we* were there when they crucified our Lord. God judges sin, says the Cross. "The wages of sin is death" (Rom. 6:23). And that Cross is a stop sign that says, "Stop sinning!" Sin is a terrible reality that will lead to death.

The Cross also tells us that "God is love" (1 John 4:8), that "he cares" (1 Peter 5:7, RSV), that "God so loved the world that he gave his only Son" for us (John 3:16, RSV).

42

A father once asked Dr. Paul Rees, "Where was God when my son was killed?" Dr. Rees tenderly replied, "Exactly where He was when his own Son was killed."

The Cross tells us that in spite of our sin and evil God still loves us. And as in faith we embrace Jesus Christ, the consequences of sin and evil are removed. Condemnation is gone. Sin is forgiven. New power and new life to choose what is right are given to us. And as the Christ who died and rose again comes into our hearts by His Holy Spirit, He begins to reshape us into the image of God and to work out God's plan in our lives.

The Cross also affirms that God is powerful and sovereign. The crucifixion was no dead end. The next event was the resurrection, the decisive proof that God overcame evil with good! The power of evil was broken, and God transformed evil into blessing. That is why the Cross tells us that God is strong enough to transform suffering to those who trust Him and who surrender their lives to Him.

How do you react to suffering? It's our reaction, not the test, which determines whether the experience blesses us or breaks us. The same sun melts butter and hardens clay. And the same suffering makes some people tender and others bitter.

There was a college student who lost his sight. He accepted his blindness as a gift from God and prayed this remarkable prayer, "Father, I thank Thee for the talent of blindness. May I so invest this talent that at the coming of the Lord Jesus He may receive His own with interest!" He was William Moon of Brighton, England, the man who invented the Moon type of raised letters for the blind that have been used in five hundred languages and put the Bible within reach of millions of people, blind people. A dedicated limitation given to God brought unlimited blessing.

The Cross calls us to follow our Lord in serving the

wretched of the earth. Our faith is not an opiate to drug us. There is a cross for each of us as God calls us to identify with the suffering of men.

God does hear when we cry. But how does He respond? He doesn't say, "Here's the answer." He says, *"Be* the answer by My grace."

We ask, "Why is there disease?"

God says, *"You* be the answer. You be a doctor or a researcher or support those who are healing."

We say, "Why is there ignorance?"

God says, *"You* be the answer. You teach."

We say, "Why is there poverty?"

God says, *"You* be the answer. Make war on poverty."

We say, "Why is there war?"

God says, *"You* be the answer. Get busy and do something to be a peacemaker."

We say, "Why is there sin?"

God says, *"You* be the answer through Jesus Christ. Receive Him as your Lord, and share Him with a world in its need."

Jesus Christ, our Lord, who had never known sin or suffering came to this world, took our sin to set us free, and now wants to love the world through you and me.

**5**

# Don't Let Your
# Conscience Be Your Guide

ONE SCHOOL OF THOUGHT holds that there are absolute standards of right and wrong, such as the Ten Commandments, that apply to all people at all times. There is another that holds that morality is a matter of doing what you feel is right; in other words, "Let your conscience be your guide."

What does the Bible teach us about this thing called conscience?

Conscience is the inner ear by which we hear the voice of God. In Romans 2:14, 15 Paul teaches that "When Gentiles who have not the law do by nature what the law requires, they are a law to themselves. . . . They show that what the law requires is written on their hearts, while their conscience also bears witness and their conflicting thoughts accuse or perhaps excuse them" (RSV).

Even though you may not have a Bible, says Paul, you do have a conscience. You can tell the difference between right and wrong because God's law is written in that conscience.

The word *conscience* literally means "to know with." It has the idea of a man being a co-witness with God for or against himself. It is as if at birth each baby had a tape recorder hung around his neck. Every time a moral decision is made by that person or someone else, it registers on that tape recorder. And at the Last Judgment the verdict on our own moral actions and those of others which we have recorded on that tape recorder will be a witness against us; it will show that we did know the difference between right and wrong.

Conscience is the soul's traffic signal; it flashes red when we do wrong and green when we do right. It's like a personal policeman who blows a whistle. It's like a judge within who passes a verdict on our actions. As Paul said, it accuses or excuses. When David sinned, records the Bible, his "heart smote him" (1 Sam. 24:5).

A Canadian Indian pictured his conscience as "a little three-cornered thing inside of me. When I do

46

wrong," he said, "it turns around and hurts me very much. But if I keep on doing wrong, it will turn so much that the corners become worn off and it doesn't hurt anymore."

From the very dawn of history conscience has been active. When Adam and Eve sinned and fell, it was conscience that made them feel guilty and led them to cover themselves with leaves. Conscience, you see, is not man-made, though it may be influenced by man. It is not simply the product of our parents' no-nos or society's taboos. Rather, conscience is a God-made, moral monitor built into our personalities.

President Garfield was once urged to take a profitable but dishonest course of action. "Nobody will ever know," he was told. His reply, "President Garfield will know, and I've got to sleep with him."

When our inner ear becomes deaf to the call of integrity, then we are in spiritual danger. How often do you tune in to ask, "What does my conscience tell me?" Oh, you've tuned in to thousands of voices—the television, the newspaper commentators, the movies, your peers, your parents, your professors. But not until you begin to listen to your inner ear can you begin to pick out God's voice.

To share the Good News of Jesus Christ with a man whose conscience is deaf is like casting pearls before swine (Matt. 7:6). A pig grubbing for food doesn't recognize the value of pearls. And a man who turns himself into an animal, wallowing in sin, ignoring the red lights that conscience flashes, can't recognize the value of the life that God offers.

Remember King Herod? He tried to silence John the Baptist. And like that you can choose to muffle your conscience. When John the Baptist rebuked the king for living with his brother's wife, the king had him thrown into prison. Now, you can try to lock your conscience up in the dark cell of your soul and throw away the key, but that's the course that leads to moral and spiritual disaster. On the other hand, you can choose to listen to your conscience, to heed its signals, and then to find through the voice of conscience that God is leading you to a new and wonderful kind of life.

However, conscience has limitations. Conscience is not an infallible guide. You may say, "I live by my conscience," and yet go very wrong. Paul once said, "I am not aware of anything against myself, but I am not thereby acquitted" (1 Cor. 4:4, RSV).

You see, conscience is a witness to whatever moral standard is fed into it. It's like a thermometer. A thermometer measures temperature, but it doesn't create it. Or you may compare conscience to a computer. Modern computers are among the most amazing machines ever invented. But a computer's output depends on the input. Feed it with the wrong information and you'll get wrong answers. The fact is that conscience is our moral computer, and we have to give it input from the right source.

For example, a gangster's conscience may tell him it's all right to kill someone but it's wrong to steal ten dollars from another gangster. Or customs and prejudices may be so strong that they seem to be the voice of God. For many years slavery and later racial segregation were tolerated by people because customs blunted their conscience. The same thing is happening with the lowering of sex standards in our day. Oswald Sanders warns that "Often when we think we are standing for principle, we are only falling for prejudice." It is only when conscience is regulated by an accurate standard that we can be sure our moral judgment is correct. We have to set our watches by standard time. And our conscience has to be set by an accurate standard, and that has been given to us in the Scriptures.

Here is a good rule, "Don't let your conscience be your guide—unless it's programmed right"—unless you have fed some input into it from the standard of the Word of God. As the psalmist said, "Thy word have I hid in mine heart, that I might not sin against thee" (Ps. 119:11).

The Bible speaks of three kinds of consciences. It speaks of a *weak* conscience. In 1 Corinthians 8:7—12 Paul writes of persons whose consciences are morbid, oversensitive, cluttered with all kinds of dos and don'ts and burdened down with man-made rules, the prisoners of taboos. And I know some Christians who live in constant depression because they have weak consciences. They feel that nothing they do is ever right.

What is the cure for this? Learn that God alone is the Lord of the conscience. Surrender your conscience to Christ. Feed your mind on God's Word. Ask the Holy Spirit to guide you. And in that surrender you can begin to discover "the glorious liberty of the children of God" (Rom. 8:21)—to do what God says, not what men tell you.

Second, there is an *evil* conscience. In 1 Corinthians 8:7 Paul speaks also of a "defiled" conscience. You see, persisting in sin will defile the conscience as dust may clog a watch. "By rejecting conscience, certain persons have made shipwreck of their faith," warned Paul (1 Tim. 1:19, RSV). Hebrews 10:22 speaks of an "evil conscience."

First Timothy 4:2 speaks of a "seared" conscience. When we habitually violate conscience, it becomes seared. Just as a hot potato may burn the mouth and make it impossible to taste, the conscience becomes insensitive to good and evil. That's why the person who says, "My conscience doesn't bother me," may be in great, serious danger, for his conscience may be nearly dead, "seared."

It is important that we feel the sensation of physical pain. Otherwise, if we got burned or hurt we'd be in danger; we wouldn't know it. We also need the moral pain of conscience in order to recognize spiritual danger. Have you tried to treat your conscience like a pet dog—you've made it sit there in a corner and be quiet? But is that "dog" growling—your conscience hurting? Then by all means heed its warning before your conscience becomes so seared that you no longer care.

And then, third, the Bible speaks of a *good* conscience. John describes it as a heart that doesn't condemn. "Beloved, if our heart condemn us not, then have we confidence toward God" (1 John 3:21). Paul describes it to Timothy as a "clear conscience" and as a "pure heart and a good conscience" (1 Tim. 3:9, 1:5, RSV). He told Governor Felix that he always took "pains to have a clear conscience toward God and toward men" (Acts 24:16, RSV).

Now, if you have a defiled or a condemning conscience, how can it be cured? What can make an evil conscience clean?

Well, it takes a double cleansing. Paul writes, "Let us cleanse ourselves from all filthiness of . . . flesh and spirit" (2 Cor. 7:1). We must separate ourselves from all known sin. That is the preparation for the second cleansing, by the blood of Christ. Hebrews 9:14 promises, "The blood of Christ" shall purify your conscience from dead works. Personally appropriate the sacrifice that Christ has made for you.

A young businessman described how Christ had liberated his conscience. For years, even though he was a professing Christian, he lived with a sense of condemnation. His life was run by guilt and the fear of God rather than by the love of God. A set of rules bound him. And then, he said, he was gripped by the truth that God had freely and completely forgiven him and that God personally loved him. He also discovered that the Holy Spirit wanted personally to direct his life. And those two truths began to revolutionize him.

He explained to me that now when he must make decisions, he waits quietly, listening with that inner ear. Often it is as if he hears two voices—the voice of the self-will saying, "Do it your way," and the voice of the Spirit of God saying, "Do it My way." When he follows the dictates of the self-will, that voice becomes louder. But the more he follows the direction of the Holy Spirit, the clearer God's voice becomes and the easier it is for him to find God's will.

But this doesn't mean that whatever my conscience tells me is God's will. Let me repeat, "Don't let your conscience be your guide—unless it's programmed right." A computer operator can't produce answers until data has been fed in. And the Holy Spirit can't guide us until God's data is fed into our minds. That's why it's so important to read, study, memorize, and fill our minds and hearts with God's inspired Word. As we fill our minds with the truths of the Bible, the data is stored there so that God's Spirit can put God's thoughts into our consciences.

Would you like to have a new conscience, a pure conscience, a clear conscience? Then take these steps:

Separate yourself from sin. Tell God about it, and make a decision by His help to make right any wrong.

Second, submit your conscience to God now, asking Him to cleanse it by the blood of Christ. And then by faith accept that God has totally, finally, and forever forgotten your sin.

And finally, surrender your conscience to let God program it. Set time every day to pray and read God's Word and definitely to seek His direction in every step, great or small. At first you may just stumble along, but as you begin to walk with Christ, you begin to learn the joy of being able to say, "The Lord is my Savior and my shepherd. . . . *He* leadeth me" (cf. Ps. 23:1, 2).

# 6

# Substitute Saviors

DRUG USE AND DRUG ABUSE have become a critical social problem. It is estimated that in the United States millions may be using marijuana and that nearly two million persons are heavily dependent on drugs. In Canada the head of the Royal Canadian Mounted Police has said that drug use is "epidemic."

A recent letter to the editor in *Time* magazine points out that the use of drugs is just a symptom. "These young folks," says the writer, "are but the children and grandchildren of the 'hollow men' of whom T. S. Eliot wrote nearly a half century ago. Turning on, tuning out, getting high or getting stoned only reflects an inner starvation and a thirst for a satisfying, fulfilling life."

That writer is correct. A man must be filled with something. If he is not filled with God, then alien forces will flood in to fill the vacuum in his soul.

Jesus Christ once told a weird and spooky story which makes just that point. He said, "When the unclean spirit has gone out of a man, he passes through waterless places seeking rest, but he finds none. Then he says, 'I will return to my house from which I came.' And when he comes he finds it empty, swept, and put in order. Then he goes and brings with him seven other spirits more evil than himself, and they enter and dwell there; and the last state of that man becomes worse than the first" (Matt. 12:43–45, RSV).

In this story Jesus compared human personality to a house with an undesirable tenant. The owner evicted the tenant, fixed up the house, and left it clean but unoccupied. One day the old tenant came walking by. He went and peered in the window and saw that no one else was living there. So he found some even wilder friends, and they broke in, took over, and completely wrecked the house and left it worse than it had been before.

When Jesus told this story, He had cast an evil spirit out of a blind and dumb man. He had been calling the people to repent and to cast sin out of their lives. Some of the religious leaders asked Jesus to give a sign to prove that He really was the Messiah. Jesus answered that only evil men would ask for further proof. But He would give them one more sign—the sign of Jonah. As Jonah was in the great fish for three days and three nights, said Jesus, so He would be in the heart of the earth for three days and three nights. He would be killed, buried, and come back to life. Then said Jesus, "The men of Nineveh shall arise against this nation at the judgment and condemn you. For when Jonah preached to them, they repented and turned to God from all their evil ways. And now a greater than Jonah is here and you refuse to believe him" (cf. Matt. 12: 38—41).

Jesus Christ brought a wonderful opportunity to the men of His day. By His death and resurrection He was making it possible for them to have a new beginning. But when they refused Jesus, when they rejected His offer of a new life, then their souls were left empty, vacant, and prey to every kind of evil.

In many ways our present generation is akin to that of Jesus' day. We too are faced with the possibility of a new life through Jesus Christ our Savior. Yet by and large men today have failed to give significant heed to the Christian faith. God has been dismissed as a superstition, Jesus Christ has been explained away as a myth, the Bible has been discarded as legend, the gospel has been laughed off as a pipe dream, the Ten Commandments have been ignored as worn-out relics, and the church has been shunted to the side as an outdated institution.

The sad story of unbelief can easily be documented. Opinion polls reflect the increasing belief of people that religion is losing its grip. What we have often failed to recognize is that unbelief has created a vacuum in the soul of modern man. But man cannot remain spiritually neutral. So as he turns from the supernatural, living God revealed in the Bible and in Jesus Christ, that vacuum has been filled with pseudo gods and substitute saviors.

One of these substitute saviors is *drugs*. Millions today are seeking to substitute drugs for God's peace. Karl Marx once said that religion was an opiate of the people. We now have men trying to make opiates into the religion of the people. The apostles of the gospel according to drugs stump the country, trying to get young people to "tune in, turn on, and drop out."

It's interesting to note that the word translated "sorcery" and "sorcerers" in the Book of Revelation actually is the Greek word which means drugs. Revelation 9:21 (RSV), for example, says that men did not "repent of their murders or their sorceries." This could mean men did not "repent of . . . their drugs"!

For many, drug use is a shortcut to peace and happiness. In an age of change, confusion, and restlessness drugs offer a kind of artificial paradise. Dr. William Nesbitt, who is a Christian psychiatrist, writes that "Modern America's reliance on drugs is unequalled in the history of mankind. People use drugs to go to sleep, drugs to make them fertile. They rely on drugs to cure them of ulcers, high blood pressure, nervousness, obesity, dandruff, and athlete's foot. No matter what ails them, they expect their doctor to have a magic drug that will cure their illnesses."

Probably no single topic causes so much concern among the parents of teenagers today as drugs. Drug use has become a leading symbol of the generation gap, and among many young people the use of drugs is the initiation rite into the fraternity of the young.

However, we sometimes overlook the fact that the greatest drug abuse may be in legal drugs and the biggest drug abusers may well be adults. A *Wall Street Journal* article tells about executives who get up early, take pep pills to race through their busy day, calm down on a martini, go to sleep on a barbiturate, and start again in the morning on a couple of diet pills.

Children who see their parents getting drunk or chain-smoking or knocking themselves out with tranquilizers won't be very impressed when their parents say, "Don't let me catch you smoking pot!"

The ultimate answer to drug abuse is not legal—it's spiritual. The peace and fulfillment we are all searching for can be found in a relationship with God that Jesus Christ can bring. He said, "Peace I leave with you, my peace I give unto you" (John 14:27); "Come unto me . . . and I will give you rest" (Matt. 11:28). These are the promises of Christ. Drug use may seem to offer an easy out, but this influence is false and temporary. Jesus Christ, on the other hand, offers a relationship with God that is true, valid, and eternal.

"Be not drunk with wine, wherein is excess," says the Bible, "but be filled with the Spirit" (Eph. 5:18). Let the genuine peace and joy of God's Spirit fill you, body and soul, and you will not have to fill that vacuum with drugs.

A second substitute savior today is *astrology,* which many have substituted for God's guidance. Astrology is an ancient belief that man's destiny is determined by his horoscope, that the plan for our lives is to be found in the pattern of the stars at the time of our birth. The Book of Daniel in the Bible mentions the astrologers in the royal court at Babylon (Dan. 4:7, 5:7). The ancient Babylonians thought that certain of the moving stars were the home of the gods. Seneca, a Roman writer, said, "On even the slightest motion of the stars hang the fortunes of the nation." Isaiah the prophet spoke of astrologers with scorn, "Let them stand forth and save you, those who divide the heavens, who gaze at the stars, who at the new moons predict what shall befall you" (Isa. 47:13, RSV).

Isn't it strange that in a day when some have rejected Christianity as a superstition, astrology has gained a new hold on the masses? Millions who never pray or read the Bible could not let a day pass without consulting their horoscopes in the paper. Astrologers have become the new priests and prophets. The phenomenon has become so widespread that *Time* magazine devoted a cover story to it. Some young couples won't set their wedding date until the astrological signs are right. On Wall Street many stock speculators tie their buying and selling to the stars. *Hair*, the hippie musical, has a company astrologer who set the date for its New York premiere.

This craze for astrology undoubtedly reflects man's search for a wisdom beyond his own. But why gaze at the stars when we can look to the One who made the stars—the Shepherd of the stars? Deuteronomy 4:19, 20 (RSV) warns: "And beware lest you lift up your eyes to heaven, and when you see the sun and the moon and the stars, all the host of heaven, you be drawn away and worship them and serve them, things which the Lord your God has allotted to all the peoples under the whole heaven. But the Lord has taken you ... to be a people of his own possession ..."

Astrology is idolatry when it attributes to planets and stars the power that belongs to God alone—when it tries to find the will of God by other means than God has appointed. Throughout the Bible, God tells us that He will guide us. "The Lord is my shepherd ... He leads me beside still waters" (Ps. 23:1, 2, RSV). "The meek will he guide in judgment; and the meek will he teach his way" (Ps. 25:9). "What man is he that feareth the Lord? him shall he teach in the way that he shall choose" (Ps. 25:12).

God guided the people of Israel through the desert by a cloud during the day and a fiery pillar at night (Exod. 13:21, 22). He guided the wise men through the stars to Bethlehem (Matt. 2:9). And He promises that if we are willing to do His will, He will guide us, too (John 7:17). He who sees the sparrow fall has a personal concern for every area of our lives (Matt: 10:29, 31). By His inspired Word, the Bible, by the teaching of His Son, Jesus Christ, by the inner leading of the Holy Spirit, He will show us and teach us His way for our lives.

When the people were converted at Ephesus, they burned their magical books (Acts 19). Almost certainly these included astrological tables. So the Christian believer has no need of astrology with its futile hints, for he turns instead to the guidance of the living God.

The third substitute savior which is so common today is *witchcraft or spiritualism*. Spiritualism has been substituted for God's resurrection power.

Again we see how superstition increases when the Christian faith is rejected. Reports from South Africa tell of wealthy white women consulting witch doctors. From California there has been a flurry of stories about Satan worship. England and Germany have had a revival of witchcraft and black magic. A German theologian has described the tremendous fascination which exists in Germany today for the world of evil spirits and black magic and how this has wrecked the mental health of some. In North America prominent clergymen who have openly rejected the miraculous elements in the Bible have taken part in seances in attempts to contact the dead.

Spiritualism claims to offer communication with the dead. This has tremendous appeal in an age when there are so many ways to die, when it has been taboo to talk about death, when men have grown skeptical about life beyond the grave, and when large sections of the Christian church have become so preoccupied with the affairs of this life that they have ceased to sound forth a triumphant and biblical hope of eternal life. Confused people, sorrowing people, grief-stricken people, have turned to those who can offer some hope, however flimsy.

According to the Bible spiritualism is both sinful and unnecessary. The crowning sin of King Saul's life came when he consulted the medium at Endor to bring back the spirit of Samuel (1 Sam. 28:7–20). Isaiah said, "And when they say to you, 'Consult the mediums and the wizards who chirp and mutter,' should not a people consult their God? Should they consult the dead on behalf of the living? To the teaching and to the testimony!" (Isa. 8:19, 20, RSV).

There is no need to go to the feeble mutterings of mediums. God has given us a clear and certain hope, "the prophetic word made more sure . . . a lamp shining in a dark place" (2 Pet. 1:19, RSV). He has "brought life and immortality to light through the gospel" (2 Tim. 1:10).

What God promises is not mere shadowy survival after death, but a resurrection to a rich and full new dimension of living. "For God has not destined us for wrath, but to obtain salvation through our Lord Jesus Christ, who died for us so that whether we wake or sleep we might live with him" (1 Thess. 5: 9, 10, RSV). For ourselves and for our loved ones who have gone on we can know that all those who trusted in Christ have gone to be with Him forever, that "eye has not seen, nor ear heard, neither has it entered into the heart of man, what God has prepared for those who love him" (cf. 1 Cor. 2:9).

# 7

# God and Man in the Space Age

MORE THAN HALF A BILLION people in thirty-three countries are estimated to have watched by satellite TV as Apollo 11 blasted off on its historic pioneer journey to the moon. One reporter who was at Cape Kennedy described the occasion as a religious experience. "The mighty thrust of the Saturn engine lifting Columbia with Eagle perched on its tip created," he said, "a biblical scene." Fire spurting, the earth trembling, the feeling he had was one of reverential awe.

Whenever I have watched the blast-off of an Apollo flight and have followed the amazing feat of astronauts working on the surface of the moon, the words of the psalmist take on new meaning. "When I look at thy heavens, the work of thy fingers, the moon and the stars which thou hast established; what is man that thou art mindful of him, and the son of man that thou dost care for him?" (Ps. 8:3, 4, RSV).

Those words were written thousands of years ago by David. As a simple country boy looking after the sheep one night, he may have leaned back on a hillside in Israel and gazed up at that moon in a starlit sky. A sense of wonder filled his soul as he thought of the greatness of God and the vastness of the universe and the smallness of man. These immortal words came flooding through him, "O Lord our Lord, how excellent is thy name in all the earth!" (Ps. 8:1).

When David looked into space, it made him worship God and question man. But today many look at space and, instead, worship man and question God. Titov, the Russian cosmonaut, said, "I don't believe in God. I believe in man who made our rockets."

Contrast this with the reaction of John Glenn, America's first man into space. Said Colonel Glenn, "The God I worship is too big for space to contain."

Astronaut James McDivitt, who orbited the earth sixty-two times aboard Gemini 4, said in a talk at the Foreign Press Club in Rome, "I didn't see God looking into my space-cabin window as I do not see God looking into my car's windshield on earth. But I could recognize His work in the stars as well as when walking among flowers in a garden. If you can be with God on earth, you can be with God in space as well." Actually, as we explore this exploding universe, we ought to have a greater sense of awe before God than David did because we know how much bigger space is and how much greater God is.

When David looked into space, it made him worship God, but it also made him ask, "What is man that thou art mindful of him, and the son of man that thou dost care for him? Yet thou hast made him little less than God, and dost crown him with glory and honor. Thou hast given him dominion over the works of thy hands; thou hast put all things under his feet" (Ps. 8:4—6, RSV).

The writer of the Book of Hebrews in the New Testament quoted this passage of David's and then added a couple of significant comments: "As it is, we do not yet see everything in subjection to him [man]. But we see Jesus . . . crowned with glory and honor because of the suffering of death, so that by the grace of God he might taste death for everyone" (Heb. 2:8, 9, RSV).

David asked, "What is man?" And today as humanity streaks into the Space Age, that question takes on a new urgency. When Apollo 10 came back, Eric Sevareid said that we ought to be more concerned about the inner nature of man than the outer nature of the universe.

These words we have quoted from the Bible give us three views of man. *First,* they show us man as God created him.

David asked God, "What is man, that You are mindful of him?" (Ps. 8:4, Amp.) In other words, he said, "When I look at this vast universe, I wonder why

You, the great God, bother to pay any attention to puny, little man."

That question is pertinent today. Man is a little cog in a gigantic, exploding universe. Isn't it sheer egotism to think that God cares for you and me? Wasn't Jesus mistaken when He said there is a heavenly Father who counts the hairs on our head (Matt. 10:30)?

Physically, man is of very little value. It is said that the average human body has enough fat to make seven bars of soap, enough sugar to sweeten seven cups of tea, enough lime to whitewash a chicken coop, enough potassium to make 2,000 matches, enough sulphur to rid a dog of fleas, enough water to take a bath in, and was worth—before inflation—about two dollars. Yet the Bible tells us that God is big enough to rule the universe and also to live within the human heart! God has a plan for the stars. God has a plan for the atom. And He has a special plan for you and me.

Notice that David said God made man a "little less than God." God made us less than Himself, but He made us like Himself. We have been made for a personal relationship with God. This is what makes man different from animals and machines. Animals have guidance mechanisms, machines have guidance mechanisms, and so do spaceships. And so does man. But we are made to be guided by the Spirit of God. And that is why one of those astronauts who weighs maybe two hundred pounds is worth more in God's sight than that great spaceship that weighs thousands of tons.

Notice also that David said God made man as His deputy, His manager, in this world. "Thou hast given him dominion over the works of thy hands; thou hast put all things under his feet."

What makes men want to explore space? Astronaut Frank Borman was asked if men would ever be found who would make the trip to Mars, which is estimated to take ten years. He said, "If the trip were physically

64

possible this moment, I could recruit a crew in ten days."

This restless, roving curiosity, this driving urge to explore, to discover, to harness the powers of the earth and the universe—where does it come from? This scientific instinct comes from God. He made us like this.

Some weeks ago I was talking with Bob Slocum, a Christian physicist who has been working on the space program. He told me about a visit he paid to Expo '67 in Montreal. As he walked through the United States Pavilion and saw the exhibition of man's accomplishments, he thought of the statement made by a French aviator which formed the theme of Expo. "To be a man," this Frenchman said, "is to feel that by one's own personal contribution one has helped to build the world."

Next Slocum came upon the display of the Mariner spacecraft on which he had worked. Perched on it was a sophisticated instrument which he had helped to design. He said that he felt a sense of pride in his soul in having been part of this project. And then he added, "I felt I would have to revise what that French aviator said, and I would have to put it this way. 'To be a man is to feel that by one's own personal contribution one has helped to build Christ's world.'" There need be no conflict between a Christian commitment and a scientific commitment. The Christian man of science knows that he is fulfilling a potential that God has built into him.

The *second* view these Bible passages show us is of man as sin has marred him. In a masterpiece of understatement the writer of Hebrews says, "We do not yet see everything in subjection to (man)." Indeed, we do not. God made this glorious man to walk with God, to love his fellow-man, to develop this world. Instead, we see man at war with God, at odds with his fellow-man, and polluting our wonderful world.

To quote Frank Borman again. When Apollo 9 came back, he said, "I now believe that technically man can do anything." That's probably true. We have the capability technologically to make a new world. But the question is, Do we have the moral and spiritual capability?

Sometimes we forget that technology gives us both the power to explore the heavens and to destroy the world. We can cure disease or wipe out entire populations. We can free enslaved millions or we can enslave millions more. A man can hate or lust or cheat just as much traveling 500 m.p.h. in a jet plane as he could traveling 10 m.p.h. in a horse and buggy.

The Bible diagnoses our problem as sin. We have been created to fulfill God's spiritual laws, just as the Apollo flights must follow certain complex laws to make it to the moon. If they disregard those laws, they will miss the moon. And the Bible says that sin is missing the mark. Instead of being God's deputies, we have tried to play God. We have tried to make up our own rules, and as a result we have missed the mark with God. We have tried to be more than men, and as a result, we have become less than men. We have pushed God out, and the empty place has been filled with hate and fear and prejudice and discord.

The *third* view these Bible passages show is of man as Christ can remake him. The writer of Hebrews says, "We do not yet see everything in subjection to (man). But we see Jesus."

Here in Jesus Christ—a Visitor from beyond space, God born in a tiny stable in Bethlehem, His birth tracked by the stars themselves—we see a new humanity. The Son of God became man that men might become the sons of God! Jesus entered creatively into history. He was not conceived as you and I were. Like Adam, He was a direct creation of God. God took dust, breathed His Spirit into it, and man began. God

66

took a virgin and breathed His Spirit into her, and a new Man began!

This Jesus held all power in His hands with perfect control. He demonstrated His perfect power by turning water into wine, multiplying a couple of loaves of bread into enough to feed thousands, walking on the water, stopping the winds. He created the laws of biology and physics and meteorology, and He could control them. And yet He never used those powers just to show off but to help others. In an age when we have more power for good or for evil than we have ever had before, we need to learn from this Son of Man how to use power.

Primarily, Jesus came to die. He came, says the Book of Hebrews, to suffer and die that "by the grace of God he might taste death for every man." He took the same nature that we have, flesh and blood, "that through death he might destroy him who has the power of death, that is, the devil, and deliver all those who through fear of death were subject to lifelong bondage" (Heb. 2:14, 15, RSV).

As Billy Graham has said, the age-old problems still exist in the space age—death, suffering, sin, selfishness. Science cannot solve these. Only the power of the blood of Christ can. And this Jesus who died rose again. He is the Christ of today—of the Space Age! He can put His new life in you. Listen to these triumphant words of the Bible, "Therefore, if any one is in Christ, he is a new creation; the old has passed away, behold, the new has come" (2 Cor. 5:17, RSV). The key is, "in Christ." By faith we can be in Christ.

Dr. Wernher von Braun, former director of the space center at Huntsville, Alabama, and the man who developed the mighty engines for the Saturn V rocket, tells the story of his own spiritual renewal. Brought up in the Lutheran church in Germany, he had abandoned the faith of his childhood by the time he became a rocket scientist in Nazi Germany. But as he saw the chaos that resulted from Hitler's dictatorship, he also saw the need for ethical values as man unleashed more and more power.

Von Braun surrendered to American forces and was taken to work at the testing site in White Sands, New Mexico. There he was impressed by the thriving spiritual life of the churches. "One day," he says, "I saw a Church of the Nazarene bus in the desert. I discovered that the pastor drove the old bus fifty miles to pick up people, and they worshiped in a wooden barracks. They reminded me of the early Christians." Meanwhile he had come to a realization of his own spiritual need, and he began to read. "The truth of Christ's teachings emerged like a revelation!" he exclaims.

Whenever von Braun travels, he reads the Gideon Bible in the hotel room. And he explains, "God has built man with curiosity. God expects man to use this gift . . . through a closer look at creation we ought to gain a better knowledge of the Creator."

# 8

# How Will the World End?

MANKIND MUST FIND global solutions to global problems or perish—if not with the bang of a nuclear holocaust, then with the whimper of a species in a civilization which ran out of air, water, resources, and food." (Mr. U Thant, former Secretary General of the United Nations)

*Time* magazine predicted, "The world will end with a cough, a wheeze, a mass gasp of emphysema."

Whether it's with a bang or a whimper, there is tremendous fascination today with the end of the world and the future of mankind.

Nearly a century has passed since Pierre Berthelot, the French scientist, was entertaining the Goncourt brothers for dinner in Paris. Berthelot began to tell them of the fantastic advances science would make in the decades ahead, the terrible weapons that would be invented. "Why," he said, "we are only beginning to lisp the alphabet of destruction. Soon science will be able to destroy the world."

There was silence around that dinner table. Then the elder Goncourt brother replied, "I think that before that happens God will come down like a great Gatekeeper, His keys dangling at His waist, and say, 'Gentlemen, it's closing time.' "

How long is it to closing time? What about the end of the world? What about the future? Are we going to blow everything up?

There are several different views of the future abroad in the world today. There are the optimists, who picture the future as an escalator going onward and upward forever—man moving by his efforts toward Utopia. But these are a tiny minority now, because two world wars and a cold war and the H-bomb and population explosion and pollution have produced many more pessimists. They see the world as a burning theater with men like puppets dangling from strings and no exits from the dilemma.

Several generations ago men ridiculed certain selections in the Bible which spoke of the possibility of the world's being destroyed, such as 2 Peter 3:10, "The day of the Lord will come like a thief, and then the heavens will pass away with a loud noise, and the elements will be dissolved with fire, and the earth and the works that are upon it will be burned up" (RSV). Today we don't laugh at such passages because they are too near to the truth.

Then we have the fatalists, who see the future as a kind of merry-go-round. History goes round in circles like the continuous showing of a movie. No beginning, no ending. Whatever has been will be. And so they say, "Don't get excited." This is the ostrich view of history, and it's like the men back in Noah's day, because Jesus said, "For as in those days before the flood they were eating and drinking, marrying and giving in marriage, until the day when Noah entered the ark, and they did not know until the flood came and swept them all away, so will be the coming of the Son of man" (Matt. 24:38, 39, RSV). In other words, said Jesus, the end of the world will come as a sudden, calamitous surprise to those who have expected everything always to be the same.

On the other hand the Communist sees the future as a kind of bolt of lightning, a zig-zag, a conflict that goes on and on. He believes that man's economic needs determine everything. You have the zig of capitalism, the zag of revolution, and finally the zig of the classless society, though he never explains why it stops there.

It's impossible really to understand the hold that communism gets on its followers unless you see that they have a kind of religious view of the future. Marx is their prophet; *Das Kapital* and the writings of Lenin, their bible; the Communist party, their messiah; revolution, their second coming; the dictatorship of the workers, their millennium; and the classless society, their heaven.

Now I believe that we who are Christians have made a serious error. The Bible has a great deal to say about the future. Jesus taught His followers what to expect in the future. Prophecy takes up approximately one-fourth of all Scripture. And yet we have soft-pedaled what the Bible says about future history. In a world longing for hope, looking for certainty, we have defaulted. A tremendously relevant and gripping part of the Christian message has been left out. I know there have been overzealous soothsayers and well-meaning but misinformed people who have gone around setting dates for the second coming of Jesus, and of course that's wrong. But that should not stop us from proclaiming what the Bible clearly says.

In Matthew 13 we find recorded an interesting story which gives us the clue to what we may expect in future history. "The Kingdom of Heaven," said Jesus, "is like a farmer sowing good seed in his field; but one night as he slept, his enemy came and sowed thistles among the wheat. When the crop began to grow, the thistles grew too. The farmer's men came and told him, 'Sir, the field where you planted the choice seed is full of thistles!' 'An enemy has done it,' he said. 'Shall we pull the thistles?' they asked. 'No,' he replied. 'You'll hurt the wheat if you do. Let both grow together until the harvest, and I will tell the reapers to gather the thistles first and burn them, and put the wheat in the barn' " (Matt. 13:24—30, LB).

Here Jesus taught that this present age was going to be an age of conflict. The wheat and the thistles will grow. Good and evil, in other words, will both thrive. And that is exactly what we see happening today—good increasing, evil increasing. In fact, we can expect that good will get better and evil will get worse in an increasing conflict until the end of history. And it's so easy to see this happening in our world today. We make a step forward, and we seem to take a step back. Just as Jesus predicted, every advance brings new problems. We invent the printing press, and it spews out pornography as well as great literature. We invent the airplane, and it drops bombs as well as carries relief supplies to hungry people.

Sometimes people ask me, "Do you believe the world is getting better or worse?" I have to answer, "Better and worse," just as Jesus predicted. It's very important to understand this. Jesus never said there would be a perfect world. He never promised that everybody would be converted to His way. Jesus did say that the gospel would be preached to all nations, but He also said that before His coming there would be wars, unbelief, a falling away from faith. He said there would be troubles and persecution.

Paul foresaw the "lawless one" being released before the day of the Lord (2 Thess. 2:8, RSV). In the last days, says the Scripture, "Evil men . . . shall wax worse and worse" (2 Tim. 3:13).

So, as David Lawrence remarked in an editorial in *U. S. News & World Report*, it is an illusion to expect permanent solutions to our problems. Why? Because man is in rebellion against God and His love and His laws.

Jesus also taught in this little story that there would be a climax to history. "The harvest," He said, would be "the close of the age" (Matt. 13:39, RSV). History today is moving inexorably toward the twenty-fifth hour—the end of all things. But the struggle will not go on endlessly. Toward the end it will grow stronger. Evil will appear to break through all restraints. But the climax will come in Christ's personal intervention and return in history. As He told His disciples on the eve of His crucifixion, "I will come again" (John 14:3).

For years newspapers in their shoptalk have referred to their largest headlines as Second Coming type. Yes, that will be the climax, the X point toward which history is moving, because the future is Christ's.

As Paul taught in Ephesians 1:9, 10 (Phillips): "God has allowed us to know the secret of his plan, and it is this: he purposes in his sovereign will that all human history shall be consummated in Christ, that everything that exists in Heaven or earth shall find its perfection and fulfillment in him." What a tremendous hope this is!

Cornelius Ryan wrote two fascinating accounts of World War II in Europe. *The Longest Day* covered D-Day when Allied Forces landed on Normandy and gained a foothold in Nazi Europe. His second book, *The Last Battle,* recounted the fall of Berlin. Now in one sense the war was over in Europe when Normandy's beaches were invaded. A decisive and fateful blow to Hitler's forces had been struck. Yet it was only after months had passed and fierce battles had been fought and tens of thousands of men had been killed that Germany finally surrendered.

Jesus' first coming was the divine D-Day. It was God's decisive invasion of history. When Jesus hung on a Cross and died, it was truly history's "longest day." What Jesus did in dying for our sins and defeating evil stretched backward and forward into eternity. That's why today if you turn your life over to Jesus Christ and receive Him by faith, you can begin a new life with forgiveness of the past and power for the future.

Jesus' Second Coming will be V-Day. There is going to be conflict between those first and second comings. But He will come in glory and great power. The "last battle" will be fought! "Then comes the end, when he delivers the kingdom to God the Father after destroying every rule and every authority and power. For he must reign until he has put all his enemies under his feet. The last enemy to be destroyed is death" (1 Cor. 15:24–26, RSV).

When a person accepts Jesus Christ as Lord and Savior, it doesn't mean all the problems will disappear, it doesn't mean all of the conflict will disappear, it doesn't mean all suffering will be taken away. But it does mean that God will give the power to live here and to share in His victory.

Jesus also taught that there would be a great crisis. The word *crisis* literally means "a separating" or "a dividing." And Jesus taught that dividing would take place at the end. In Matthew 13:40–32 (LB) He said, "Just as in this story the thistles are separated and burned, so shall it be at the end of the world: I will send My angels and they will separate out of the Kingdom every temptation and all who are evil, and throw them into the furnace and burn them. There shall be weeping and gnashing of teeth. Then the godly shall shine as the sun in their Father's Kingdom." And He said, "Let those with ears, listen!" In other words, Jesus said, "Be prepared. Be ready. Pay attention. Realize what's going to come. Get ready for that crisis."

Paul, speaking to the philosophers on Mars' hill in Athens, emphasized the same truth. He told them that God "has set a day for justly judging the world by the man He has appointed, and has pointed Him out by bringing Him back to life again" (Acts 17:31, LB).

In other words, Jesus Christ now is the Savior who says, "Come unto me, all . . . (who) labor and are heavy laden, and I will give you rest" (Matt. 11:28). He invites you to come to Him and find His abundant life today. But someday that same Christ is going to be the Judge of all men. That Day of Judgment may seem to be a long way off now. But even now you and I are making the choices and decisions which then are going to be revealed.

Several years ago during an eclipse of the sun, a teenager in Indiana ignored her parents' warning and gazed out the window at the eclipse for about five minutes. She felt nothing. It appeared that nothing had happened to her eyesight at first. Later that day as she was walking downtown, things began to blur and soon she was in total darkness. The results of her carelessness were not immediately evident, but later they showed up.

Thankfully in the case of that young lady, what the doctors thought was irreversible damage was later changed, and her sight returned. But for those who continually and without repentance refuse the mercy and love of God, there will be a final and eternal judgment.

When will this crisis be? I don't know. And Jesus told us not to speculate needlessly. There are signs in the world that are being fulfilled that might point to the end of the age coming near. But we can't be sure. Jesus said, "In an hour when you think not the Son of man will come" (cf. Matt. 24:44).

The Second Coming of Christ and the end of the age are not subjects for idle curiosity. The hope of Christ's return is no escapist clause. It's not an out for Christian complacency nor an alibi for noninvolvement. To the contrary, it's a spur to holiness, to evangelism, and to obedience. It's a motivation to make God's work on earth our own, for as Jesus said, "Occupy till I come" (Luke 19:13). But it's also a motivation to be ready. "For in such an hour as you think not the Son of man will come." And it's a motive to be holy. The Scripture says, "Abide in him that when he comes we may not be ashamed" (cf. 1 John 2:28).

As Martin Luther said of himself, "We are to believe and live and love and work as though Jesus Christ died yesterday, rose today, and is coming again tomorrow."

# 9

# The Buck Stops Here

WILL ROGERS ONCE SAID that the history of America will be written in three phases: the passing of the Indian, the passing of the buffalo, and the passing of the buck.

Today we urgently need people who are willing to say, "The buck stops here. I will take responsibility for my life, my home, my nation."

The Bible tells us that when God freed the people of Israel from slavery in Egypt, one of the first things He taught them was a sense of responsibility. The Lord called Moses to the top of Mount Sinai and said, "I am the Lord your God. I brought you out of Egypt, out of bondage. You shall have no other gods before me" (cf. Exod. 20:2, 3). Then He chiseled out the Ten Commandments for Moses.

"I have freed you," the Lord was saying. "I have made you My people. Now you have a responsibility to listen to Me and to obey My word." No responsibility, no freedom.

While the Lord was talking to Moses, the people became impatient, at the foot of the mountain. They said to Aaron, Moses' brother, "Up, make us gods, who shall go before us; as for this Moses, the man who brought us up out of . . . Egypt, we do not know what has become of him" (Exod. 32:1, RSV). So Aaron said to the people, "Bring me your gold earrings," and he melted them down, shaped the molten gold into the figure of a calf, and said to the people, "Here is your god!" (cf. Exod. 32:2–4).

When Moses came down and saw what had happened, he was furious. He smashed the tablets on which the Ten Commandments were written and destroyed the golden calf. Then in blazing fury he turned to Aaron and demanded, "Why did you do this?"

Aaron was a timid and weak man. So instead of saying, "I did wrong; I am responsible," he said, "Don't be angry with me. The people were set on doing evil. They said, 'Make us gods.' So I just took their gold and threw it into the fire, and out came this calf" (cf. Exod. 32:19—24).

"Don't blame me," says Aaron. "I'm not responsible. It's their fault. Blame the furnace if you want to. The fire did it."

Aaron was a thoroughly modern man. He wouldn't take the rap; he wouldn't shoulder responsibility. Society was at fault. The furnace was to blame, not Aaron. As Phillips Brooks once said, "There never was a speech more true to our human nature. We are all ready to lay the blame upon the furnace."

The Nazi war criminals said, "We were just following orders. We didn't really want to kill the Jews. But Hitler made us do it. Don't blame us."

The criminal says, "I'm the product of the neighborhood I was brought up in. Don't blame me; blame the environment."

The alcoholic says, "My problem is a psychological hang-up from my childhood. Don't blame me."

The rioter in the streets says, "I've been looted, so now I'm going to loot. Don't blame me."

The bigot says, "Well, I'm really not prejudiced, personally, but I've got to go along with my friends. Don't blame me."

The student who cheats or indulges in promiscuous sex says, "Everybody else is doing it. Why expect me to be different?"

The businessman who chisels on his expense account says, "It's just the way the system works. Don't blame me."

Now, of course, society often *is* guilty. Take a child raised in a brutal home in a rat-infested slum or a child raised in a loveless home in an affluent society; he has been sinned against. And if that child goes wrong, a lot of people must share the blame. But it's a dangerous delusion when we make collective guilt the scapegoat for personal responsibility—when the drunk who kills in an accident is no longer a sinner but just a sick man; the criminal is no longer guilty but just the victim of his environment; children are no longer accountable for their misdeeds but merely the product of their homes.

In "Peanuts," Lucy was once explaining to Charlie Brown that children really shouldn't be punished when they did wrong, that their parents were to blame. "But Lucy," said Charlie, "did you ever stop to think that parents had parents?"

We all play the game of "Denial." We evade responsibility, shrug off guilt, blame someone else for our problems. And it all started in the Garden of Eden. Adam ate the forbidden fruit, and God called him to account. But Adam said, "I'm not responsible. The woman You gave me, remember her? Well, she gave me fruit of the tree, and I ate it. Don't blame me; it's Eve's fault." Then God asked Eve, "What have you done?" and she said, "It's not my fault. The serpent beguiled me, and I ate" (cf. Gen. 3:12, 13).

But God held them all responsible! To the serpent He said, "Because you have done this, you are cursed!" (Gen. 3:14). To Eve He said, "I will greatly multiply your pain in childbearing." To Adam He said, "Because you have listened to the voice of your wife, and have eaten of the tree of which I commanded you, 'You shall not eat of it,' cursed is the ground because of you. ... In the sweat of your face you shall eat bread till you return to the ground, for out of it you were taken; you are dust, and to dust you shall return" (Gen. 3:16, 17, 19, RSV).

Adam and Eve started something that has never stopped. Their son Cain killed his brother Abel (Gen. 4:8). And when the Lord said to Cain, "Where is Abel your brother?" Cain replied, "I do not know; am I my brother's keeper?" (Gen. 4:9, RSV). The same old, tired refrain, "Don't blame me; who said I was responsible for him?"

But again God would not let him off the hook. The

Lord said, "The voice of your brother's blood is crying to me from the ground. And now you are cursed . . . you shall be a fugitive and a wanderer on the earth" (Gen. 4:10–12, RSV).

Sin turns us all into latter-day versions of Adam and Eve and Cain. Sin makes us God-evaders, truth-evaders, responsibility-evaders. The capitalist blames the Communist for the problems of the world, and the Communist blames the capitalist; the black man blames the white man, and the white man blames the black; parents blame children, children blame parents; wife blames husband, husband blames wife. No one wants to say, "Lord, is it I? Am I what's wrong with the world? Am I what's wrong with my home? Am I the trouble in this fouled-up relationship?"

Dr. William Parker, psychologist and author, notes that psychology is moving back to the biblical belief in responsibility. He writes, "Psychology is beginning to insist on people's assuming responsibility for thoughts, feelings, and behavior."

Viktor Frankl, the famous psychiatrist, says that the founding fathers of America made a mistake, in his view, when they talked about "life, liberty, and the pursuit of happiness." In his opinion, they should have said, "Life, liberty, and the discharge of responsibility."

Now God will not let us evade responsibility. Paul says in Romans 14:12 (RSV), "Each of us shall give account of himself to God." Man is not a zero. You are not a zero. Our choices are important. God does not force us to believe. He does not force us to obey. But He does hold us responsible for our decisions. Hell itself is the greatest monument to human responsibility that we must finally account for our actions.

To be responsible means to respond, to give an answer. God doesn't make animals or machines give an account of themselves. But we are made in God's image. That means God can speak, and we can answer. God can command, and we can say yes or no. So God makes us give an answer for what we do with His Lordship of our lives. He requires an answer for what we do with our lives. He asks an answer for what we do with our brother. And above all He demands an answer for what we do with Jesus Christ.

What was history's ultimate act of irresponsibility? I believe it was when Pontius Pilate sentenced Jesus Christ to die—when Jesus Christ laid down His life for you and me.

As dawn licked at an eastern sky, Jesus Christ was brought before Pilate, the Roman governor, and accused by some Jewish leaders of various crimes (Luke 23:1, 2). Pilate wanted no part of their quarrel. He tried to duck out from the responsibility. "And when he learned that he belonged to Herod's jurisdiction, he sent him over to Herod." But Jesus would not answer Herod's questions (Luke 23:7, 9, RSV). Then Pilate said to the Jewish leaders, "Take him yourselves and judge him by your own law." But they answered, "It is not lawful for us to put any man to death" (John 18:31, RSV).

Pilate questioned Jesus. He became convinced that He was innocent of any crime. Then he thought of a brilliant solution. He went out to the people and said, "I find no crime in him. But you have a custom that I should release one man for you at the Passover. Do you want me to release Barabbas, the murderer, or Jesus?" And they shouted back, "Barabbas" (cf. Luke 23:33–40).

"Pilate said . . . 'Then what shall I do with Jesus who is called Christ?' They all said, 'Let him be crucified.' And he said, 'Why, what evil has he done?' But they shouted all the more, 'Let him be crucified'" (Matt. 27:22, 23, RSV).

Pilate kept trying to evade. But he couldn't. The decision was his. No one else could make it for him. So "he took water and washed his hands before the crowd," seeking to remove from his hands the guilt he could never wipe from his soul. "Then he released for them Barabbas and . . . delivered (Jesus) to be crucified" (Luke 27:24, 26, RSV).

Pilate ran away from his responsibility, but he could not make Jesus run away, for Jesus died willingly. In the ultimate act of responsibility Jesus Christ took our sins and bore *our* sins in His own body on the Cross. God was saying in the death of Jesus, "I have taken responsibility for your sins. I have come in Jesus Christ and put all your guilt to His account. Now I am responsible for you." "He was wounded for our transgressions, he was bruised for our iniquities. . . . All we like sheep have gone astray; we have turned every one to his own way; and the Lord has laid on him the iniquity of us all" (Isa. 53:5, 6, RSV).

Does this seem like a spiritual cop-out? Does it seem like passing the buck to God? Does it seem like the easy way out?

Strangely enough, it's only in the light of that Cross, only when we see that God didn't wash His hands of us, only when we see that God didn't cop-out on His sinful creatures, only when we see that God has become responsible for us, that you and I can really become responsible again.

Jesus told a story once about a boy who ran away from responsibility. But, "When he came to himself," he went home to his father and said, "Father, *I* have sinned . . ." (Luke 15:17, 21). He didn't say, "Father, you're to blame." He didn't say, "My friends led me astray." He didn't say, "My older brother picked on me." No, he said, "Father, I have sinned. I am responsible." And his father threw his arms around him and said, "My son was dead, and is alive again; he was lost, and is found" (Luke 15:24).

You see, when a man turns to God, he finds himself. He begins to live responsibly before God with all he is and all he has. He learns to say, "I'm not responsible just to myself. I am my Father's son. I am my brother's brother."

He learns to take responsibility for his sins. Instead of blaming others for his mistakes, he learns to say, "It's my fault. I was wrong. I am sorry."

He learns to take responsibility for his life—to find out what his gifts are and to make use of them; to make decisions, yet not be afraid to change them when he has to; to give his word and to keep it.

He learns to take responsibility for others—to help them bear their own burdens and to share the weight.

He is free from the awful responsibility of pretending he is God when he is not and from the irresponsibility of pretending he is not a man when he is. He is learning that there are some burdens he can cast only on the Lord and some he must carry in the Lord's strength.

Some day Pilate will stand in front of God, for the Bible says, "It is appointed unto men once to die, but after this the judgment" (Heb. 9:27). Once Pilate asked, "What shall I do with Jesus?" Then he will be asking, "What will Jesus do with me?"

Some day we will stand there too. Alone. As distinct as when we were born. As alone as when we die. We will not be able to claim or blame our environment, our schooling, our upbringing, our neighborhood. God will know all about that. We will stand totally responsible to God on this account, "What did you do with Jesus Christ?" Some day we will have to answer.

**10**

# Jesus, Yes!

EVEN THOUGH ORGANIZED RELIGION seems to have lost its drawing power, there is still a tremendous fascination today with the Person of Jesus Christ. Many of the hippies speak of their sandals as "Jesus' boots." as if subconsciously identifying with Him. A hit song not long ago said, "Jesus is a soul Man, and I'm sold on Him." Many of these people may not understand Jesus. They may not fully grasp that He is the Son of God. But there is a magnetism that continues to draw them to Christ.

Some time ago I met a student at the University of North Carolina who was a new Christian. He said that his friends accuse Christians of living in luxury while some people have no shoes. In response he said, "That may be true of some professing Christians, but what do you have against Jesus?" To that they had no reply.

From the very beginning Jesus had this tremendous power to attract men. Matthew, the tax agent, was in his office bending over a tax form when Jesus apparently just walked in and said, "Follow Me." And Matthew got up and did just that (Matt. 9:9). On the spot he threw over a lucrative racket for a gigantic question mark.

How come? How do you explain the magnetism of Jesus? Not by His human background, certainly. He was born into a poor family and never owned anything except His clothing. He never traveled beyond the limits of His own small country and He had little training or formal education.

Jesus can't be explained by His followers. A man who is trying to start a great movement usually seeks out authorities, experts, powerful men, to be his assistants. But not Jesus. He took ordinary men—small businessmen, fishermen, civil servants—who had no greatness when He called them, but in His company and shadow they became great.

And think of His influence. One writer describes it this way, "Nineteen wide centuries have come and gone and today He is the centerpiece of the human race and the leader of the column of progess. I am far within the mark when I say that all the armies that ever marched, and all the navies that ever were built, and all the parliaments that ever sat, and all the kings that ever reigned, put together have not affected the life of man upon this earth as powerfully as has that One Solitary Life"—Jesus of Nazareth.

A nationally known authority has said that one reason young people are turning to drugs is that there is no charismatic personality to lead them, to call them to commitment. Well, I am convinced there is—that Jesus Christ has every quality we need in a leader. I think that the best description I ever heard of a true leader is that he must possess three attributes: the understanding of a psychiatrist, the sympathy of a nurse, and the toughness of a sergeant. And all of these are exemplified to the ultimate degree in Jesus Christ.

First, He understands men. Jesus had an insight into human nature greater than any psychiatrist. He displayed an amazing ability to read men's hearts. Once He healed a sick man and said that his sins were forgiven. Some of the scribes were shocked, and they silently asked themselves, " 'Why does this man talk such blasphemy? Who can . . . forgive sins but God?' Jesus realized instantly what they were thinking, and said to them, 'Why must you argue like this in your minds?' " (Mark 2:7, 8, Phillips).

Again one day Jesus talked with a Samaritan woman by a well. In the course of their conversation He told her to go and call her husband. She answered, "I have no husband." And Jesus replied, "You are right. You have had five husbands and the man you now have is not your husband at all." The woman went back to her neighbors and said, "Come . . . see the man who told me everything I've ever done!" (cf. John 4:7—18, 28, Phillips).

Jesus' insight led Him to recognize the flaw in human nature. John's Gospel tells us that at the beginning of Jesus' ministry, ". . . Many believed in him as they saw the signs that he gave. But Jesus . . . did not trust himself to them—for he knew them all. He did not need anyone to tell him what people were like . . ." (John 2:23–25, Phillips). "He himself could tell what was in a man." He knew their faith was superficial and temporary. He knew that man's inner being is ruled by evil principle and man needs to be changed. Jesus knew you could not build a new world on the cracked foundation of human nature. Former Ambassador George Kennan is right when he says, "The decisive seat of evil . . . is not in social and political institutions . . . but simply in the weakness and imperfection of the human soul itself." And that's what Jesus saw.

But Jesus also knew the potential that lay within men. When He called that blustering fisherman, Simon Peter, He said, "I know you. You are Simon, but you shall be Peter" (cf. John 1:42). Simon was an unstable character, but by the grace of Jesus he would become Peter, the "rock man." Peter stumbled; Peter fell; Peter made mistakes. But he stayed with Jesus, and Jesus made him into a superb Christian.

Luther Burbank, the famed horticulturist, once said, "Every weed potentially is a flower." Jesus Christ looks at men the way Luther Burbank looked at weeds. "Every sinner potentially is a saint." And out of the failure and tangles of life Jesus Christ can bring pardon and peace and purpose.

But Jesus Christ also deserves to be our Leader because of the tenderness that characterizes Him. There are some people who have great insight into human nature, but they are cynics. So they can never lead or challenge or inspire anybody. But not so with Jesus.

For many years it has been thought manly not to cry. Men who wanted to appear very masculine bottled their emotions up inside them. But Jesus shows us that it is the strong who can truly cry. He wept when His friend

Lazarus died (John 11:35). He wept over the city of Jerusalem that had rejected God's grace (Luke 19:41).

Jesus could show scathing anger at the religious phonies of His day. But He had nothing but tenderness to show for those who suffered and for those who repented of their sins. To the woman taken in adultery He said, "Neither do I condemn you; go, sin no more" (cf. John 8:11). He was moved with compassion over the hungry and sick—enough to do something about it. He was tender enough to allow Himself to be nailed to a cross to bear the sins of a world that had rejected Him and in His dying words to say, "Father, forgive them; for they know not what they do" (Luke 23:34).

The Bible teaches that this Christ is not one ". . . who is unable to sympathize with our weaknesses, but one who in every respect has been tempted as we are, yet without sinning. Let us then with confidence draw near to the throne of grace, that we may receive mercy and . . . grace to help in the time of need" (Heb. 4:15, 16, RSV). Here is a leader—one who can help us when we hurt, forgive us when we've sinned, pick us up when we fall, and teach us the meaning of compassion for a broken and a bleeding world.

The third great leadership quality of Jesus was His strength. He was as tough as any top sergeant. He didn't pamper men. He demanded of them, and He brought out the best in them. Jesus refuses to let us settle for second best. He makes demands of us so that He may bring out our best for God and ourselves and others.

Jesus was tender, but He was also tough—tough-minded, tough-bodied, tough-willed, tough-souled. He was tough with Himself. His body was strong from long marches during the days and sleeping under the stars at night. He set His face toward Jerusalem, knowing He was going to suffer there on the Cross, and nothing could swerve Him (Luke 9:51). There was a toughness in His spirit. And Jesus made similar demands of His

89

followers. He didn't soft-soap them. He didn't hide His scars to win a crowd. Instead He said, "If any man will come after me, let him deny himself, and take up his cross, and follow me" (Matt. 16:24). He said there was going to be hardship and rejection and suffering for His followers. He demanded that they seek first God's kingdom (Matt. 6:33) and put everything else aside for the cause. Total commitment is what He demanded because He made a total commitment for us.

So here is this magnificent Jesus—more understanding than a psychiatrist, more sympathetic than a nurse, tougher than a Marine sergeant. But the good news is that Jesus isn't a dead Teacher from the dim, dark past. He is a living Lord. He promised when He left this earth, "I will not leave you alone. I will send you as My Representative the Holy Spirit—another Counselor, another Leader" (cf. John 14:16–8, RSV). And through the Holy Spirit, Jesus Christ still says, "Follow Me into this twentieth century world. Follow Me into IBM, follow Me into the TV studio, follow Me into the home, follow Me onto the campus, and I'll be your teacher."

I heard of a student who said, "I can't stomach this stuff about Jesus being our Savior and shedding His blood for us." He continued, "I believe Jesus was a great Man. I'll be glad to follow Him as my Leader, but I don't need a Savior."

A friend replied, "You want to follow Jesus? Okay, let's take the first step. Who was it the Bible says was found without sin?" The student thought a moment and then said, "It was Jesus. And I can't follow Him; I'm not good enough." And his friend said quietly, "You see, we don't need a Leader first; first, we need a Savior."

As the Scripture says, "Christ also suffered for you, leaving you an example, that you should follow in his steps. He committed no sin. . . . He himself bore our sins in his body on the tree, that we might die to sin and live to righteousness" (1 Pet. 2:21, 22, 24, RSV).

Some would say of Jesus today, "I will have Him as a Leader but not as a Savior." To such Jesus says, "I died for you. First, come to My Cross; then follow in My steps and make Me your Lord."

Some would say, "I believe in Jesus as my Savior, but I want to be my own Lord." To such Jesus says, "But I died to be Lord. You cannot trust Me as Savior and not follow Me as Lord."

# 11

# Is the Church on the Way Out?

ON EVERY HAND TODAY the voices of doom are sounding the death knell of the Christian church. A Canadian bishop made headlines a while back when he predicted that the church has only ten more years to live.

Malcolm Muggeridge, the British writer, is a recent convert to Christianity. Yet he too believes the church may be on its deathbed. Says Muggeridge, "I am personally convinced that our Western civilization is approaching its end.... The Christian church is inevitably involved in this death of our civilization.... I have a pessimistic view of the future of the church."

Today there is a widespread feeling of disillusionment with the church as we know it. Billy Graham said recently that young people today are attracted to Jesus Christ but are often turned off by the church. He observes that when students come forward in his crusades, they are with him until he says, "Now if you're going to grow in the Christian life, you need to get into the church." At that point, he says, he can see some of them change expression as if to say, "You just lost me. I can't see that the church is important."

Many of the radical theologians today are saying that we should scuttle the church and get into the world where the action is. But we can't simply dump the church. I believe the church has many critics but no rivals when it comes to redeeming men and serving God. The church has a vital role in God's plan. God is at work in this world to bring about a spiritual revolution, and the church is His revolutionary community. Jesus Christ said, "I will build my church; and the gates of hell shall not prevail against it" (Matt. 16:18). He pictures the church both as a citadel that cannot be demolished and an army that cannot be resisted.

Jesus Christ came to give His life for individuals, but He also came to give His life for the church. The same Paul who said, "(Christ) loved me, and gave Himself for me" (Gal. 2:20), also said, "Christ . . . loved the church, and gave Himself for (the church)"

94

(Eph. 5:25). We may come to Jesus Christ one by one; but when we come to Him, we become part of His family. Salvation apart from the church is a contradiction. Acts 2:47 tells us that "The Lord added to the church daily those who were being saved."

The influence of the Christian church in our world isn't primarily a matter of numbers. Christians are a minority in the world, and according to Jesus, we always will be. Yet minority movements are important for they always cast the shadow of the future. The Nazis were a minority in Germany until Hitler took over. Communists were always a minority in Russia until the revolution. And just a handful of Christians reshaped the course of the Roman Empire.

On the day of Pentecost there were only three Christians in Palestine for every 100,000 people. That would be as if there were only 6,000 Christians in the entire United States today. Yet those first Christians had such power that even their enemies conceded they "have turned the world upside down" (Acts 17:6).

Now numbers *are* important. Luke records in the Book of Acts that 3,000 were converted on the day of Pentecost when Peter preached (Acts 2:41). We shouldn't despise numbers, yet neither should we idolize them. As Elton Trueblood once said, "What matters is neither the presence of crowds nor the absence of crowds, but a new creature in Christ Jesus."

The crucial question isn't, How big is the church? It's, What *is* the church?

Picture in your mind a street corner with four buildings on it: a bank, a bar, a theater, and a church. Everyone knows what a bank is for. Everyone understands what a bar is for—and a theater. But how many people really understand what a church is and what it is for?

In the Bible the church is not a building nor a program nor a budget. The church may use these things. But the church is people—God's redeemed people.

Jesus showed this at the very start of His ministry. Part of His strategy was to gather together a group of twelve men. He chose twelve because there were twelve tribes of Israel in the Old Testament, and Jesus had come to start God's new people. Jesus chose these men at a time when the crowds that came to hear Him were growing but the opposition was hardening. He wanted them to continue His work after He was gone and to deepen and to spread it.

Mark's Gospel tells us that three things marked these twelve men. First, they had a *personal commitment to Christ.* Mark 3:13 says Jesus called "whom he would: and they came to him."

Second, they had a *unique fellowship in Christ.* Included were men of different temperaments and backgrounds: boisterous Peter and quiet John; Simon the Zealot, a member of the underground, a revolutionary; and Matthew, the tax collector, who was a member of the establishment and worked for the Roman government. Before they met Jesus, Simon would gladly have slit Matthew's throat. But when Jesus accepted them, they accepted each other.

Third, they had a *clear mission for Christ.* Mark says that Jesus called them to "be with him," to have personal fellowship with Him, but also to send them out to preach and heal and cast out demons. He had a job for them to do.

I am convinced that the contemporary church will never regain its influence until we recover these distinctives that marked Jesus' first disciples. Far too many church members have only a secondhand, environmental faith. They go to church because it's part of their culture. As someone said, they have "oozed" into church membership without ever having made a personal commitment to Jesus Christ. Then when they go off to college or when they move away, they leave the church behind. They are said to have "lost their faith," but in many cases there was no personal commitment to Jesus Christ to begin with.

In the United States today about 65 percent of the population goes to some church. But in California and Oregon and Washington that percentage drops to 15 and 20 percent. Why? Part of the reason may be that people have moved to the West Coast from the East and the South and the Midwest, where the church has always been at the center of the community affairs. They have gone to church because it was the expected thing. But when these same people move West, where churchgoing isn't the expected thing, they become spiritual drop-outs because of a lack of an inner commitment.

I've often heard it said that to be a church member is far easier than to be a member of a service club or a country club. In one sense it should be. The church is not a club; it's for everyone. But we need to make it clear that there are demands if we are to belong to Christ's church. It demands a belief in Christ and a *commitment to Christ.*

Jesus took His men aside one day to a mountain and He asked them, "Who do you say I am?" Peter answered, "You are . . . the Son of the living God." And Jesus said, "On this rock I will build my church" (Matt. 16:15, 16, 18, RSV). The foundation of the church would be Jesus Christ Himself, the solid Rock, and on Him would be built those who confessed with Peter that He was the Son of God and the Savior of the world.

Then Jesus said, "If any man will come after me, let him deny himself, and take up his cross, and follow me" (Matt. 16:24). In other words, the true Christian is willing to put Christ first in his life.

I have a friend who is the pastor of a fast growing church in North Carolina. A fine young couple, the man a graduate of West Point, started to attend this church and said they wanted to become members, so my

97

friend made an appointment to visit in their home. He told them that joining the church involved a costly commitment. He also explained what it meant to be a Christian and what would be expected of them. At the end of two hours the man said, "I'm not ready to join your church. I never realized before what it meant and what it took to be a Christian. Let me think about it."

Several weeks later the young man said, "Now I am prepared to give my life to Christ." Today he is a faithful, effective member of that church and a genuine follower of Christ. But he never would have been unless someone made clear to him that he had to commit his life to Christ wholeheartedly.

It is also vital today that our churches be able to give a convincing demonstration of what *fellowship in Christ* can be. When I was a boy in Canada, we used to go every summer to a conference where the motto was, "All one in Christ Jesus." That should describe our churches, but does it?

This world today is hungry for a real sense of community. Psychiatrist Rollo May says that the 400,000 young people who went to the Woodstock festival at Bethel, New York, showed that youth is yearning for a sense of community. Can they find at your church and my church a real Bethel, a real "house of God," the sense of belonging they were looking for at the rock festival?

Dr. Richard Halverson says Christian fellowship is more than serving Kool-Aid in the church basement. Christian fellowship isn't a bunch of people in a room bouncing off each other like Ping-Pong balls; it's like grapes crushed together. It means sharing our lives with each other.

The church ought to be a place where people are accepted because of Jesus Christ, whatever their bank account, whatever their haircut, whatever the color of their skin! At the New York Graham Crusade I looked down the platform one night. On the same row where I

98

was sitting were three friends of mine—one Italian, one black, one Jewish—all Christians. We sat there together, singing, praying, worshiping, loving God and Christ. I thought, "This is what the church should be, the place where black is beautiful and brown is beautiful and even white is beautiful because of Jesus Christ." Do people sense that when they come to your church and mine—that we want them because of Christ?

Finally, we need to understand that the entire church has a *mission for Christ*. Jesus called those twelve men not only to be with Him but also to go for Him. Just as our Lord Jesus Christ "came not to be ministered unto, but to minister, and to give his life . . . for many" (Mark 10:45), so we who are His followers are called to lose our lives for the sake of others. The church is the only organization in the world that does not exist for the sake of its members. The church exists to bring to all men the message of Christ. It is both the bride of Christ to worship Him and the body of Christ to work for Him. The church is not just an end; it is a means, a channel, through which God loves the world.

You see, the church is not like an athletic association, where the spectators attend a game, sit in the stands, pay the players, and cheer them on. The church is like a team, where everyone plays and everyone participates. And the pastor is supposed to be the coach who trains the team and helps everyone to make a contribution. Paul says that God gives to the church pastors and teachers and evangelists, not to do all of God's work but to train and equip God's people for the work of ministry (Eph. 4:11, 12). Every Christian has some gift which the Holy Spirit gives to use for the good of the whole team. In 1 Corinthians Paul says, "There are varieties of gifts, but the same Spirit. . . . In each of us the Spirit is manifested in one particular way, for some useful purpose" (1 Cor. 12:4, 7, NEB).

Throughout the world today the movements which are growing fastest are those which put their entire membership to work to spread their beliefs. The Christian church will never reach the whole world with the gospel as long as we leave the task only to the pastors and evangelists and missionaries. Only when every Christian acts by words and deeds to make Christ known will we be able to carry out His great command to "preach the gospel to every creature" (Mark 16:15).

One month after President Kennedy was assassinated, a memorial service was held at Arlington National Cemetery. In the dusk of that December evening someone lit a candle from the flame over his grave. That candle lit another and another and another until there were thousands of candles being carried away, flickering like fireflies on the bridge back to Washington and out into the Virginia countryside.

When we go to worship God on Sunday, it should be like that. The end of worship should signal the beginning of witness and service. We light our lives afresh at the eternal flame of Jesus Christ, then carry that flame back into the darkness and let our lights shine for Jesus Christ in our homes and schools and businesses that week. Here is the church as God meant it to be, not an anemic, hidebound, harmless institution, but Christ's body, Christ's army, Christ's people—with a great calling to be committed to Him, with a great fellowship to demonstrate in Christ, and with a great task to carry out for Christ in this world.

**12**

# To Whom Shall We Go?

TWENTY YOUNG PEOPLE in England were polled on their religious opinions. One question was, "Do you think that God understands radar?" And eighteen of the twenty gave no as their first reaction! Those young people had a picture of God as out-of-date, as an old fogy living some place back in the nineteenth century.

I have talked with many people who just don't see how God can make any difference in our everyday problems. "What's the use," they say, "of a church on its knees praying for lost souls while a blinding population explosion dooms a hundred thousand new babies every day to slow starvation? What good is it for a vast throng to jam a stadium and listen to a sermon while festering wounds of racial hatred blister the hide of humanity? Isn't it worse than useless to take a man off and ask him if he's 'saved' while a terrifying arms race spawns mass terror weapons?"

To many modern critics the gospel is like an antique chair in a museum. It's a curious relic of the past—interesting to study, but you wouldn't dream of sitting on it.

The secularist says that we no longer need God to fill the gaps in our knowledge. The Communist says that religion is an opiate which has no place in the socialist state. The sophisticate admits that faith may be all right for children but is excess baggage for grown-ups.

During World War I the French General Gallieni offered a plan to save Paris. He planned to strike the right flanks of the German army by using the vehicles of Paris to carry his troops to the front. But first he had to obtain permission from the commander, General Foch. One day he came to his superior's camp clad in an old, out-of-date uniform. Since General Foch was absent, a subordinate dismissed him curtly.

Later he told General Foch of the visitor and said that his name was Gallieni. In anger General Foch demanded why such a great general had been treated so badly, and the aide replied, "Who would take seriously an old man dressed up like that?"

"That old man," said Foch, "had a plan that could save the city of Paris and the lives of a million men!"

Today, Jesus Christ comes with a plan that can save the world. But because He comes dressed in the garb of the first century, many have dismissed Him.

When people say that Jesus Christ is not relevant to our modern problems, that is not a new accusation. People said that during His lifetime. The Gospel of John tells about a great crowd that was following Jesus one day because they had seen His miracles. Jesus took some loaves and fishes from a little boy and fed them from this tiny lunch. Then the people tried to seize Jesus and make Him their king. But when Jesus realized what they were trying to do, He withdrew to the hills by Himself.

Jesus declined to be king on their terms. If He had wanted to, He could have started a popular uprising against Rome. But He refused to be "relevant" in their terms. Why? As William Barclay says, "They wished to use Him for their own purposes, to mold Him to their own dreams. They were looking for a Messiah who would be king and conqueror, who would set His foot upon the eagle's neck and drive the Romans from Palestine, who would change Israel from a subject nation to a world power."

"What a king He'd make!" they thought. "Let's harness His power to our plans and our purposes!" That attitude still lingers today. There are many people who would like to make Jesus into a modern revolutionary. We want Christ's gifts without His Cross. We want to use Christ instead of allowing Him to use us. Our humanistic, man-centered age still thinks more of what we want than of what God wants. You see, the real question is not, Is Jesus Christ relevant to my life? but, Is my life relevant to the purposes of Christ?

When Jesus withdrew, the crowd followed Him to the other side of the lake. Then He said something very significant: "Truly . . . I say to you, you seek me, not because you saw signs"—not because you understand who I am and why I have come—"but because you ate your fill of the loaves. Do not labor for the food which perishes, but for the food which endures to eternal life, which the Son of man will give to you" (John 6:26, 27, RSV).

What a sharp contrast there is here between the quest of the crowd and the mission of Christ. The crowd wanted life. Christ was there to give them life. What was the difference? It was in the interpretation of what makes up life.

"Life," they said, "comes when we are fed. Life comes when our stomachs are full. Life comes when our physical needs are satisfied." Many people still think that way. A great deal of the talk of making Christianity relevant is two thousand years old. It assumes that nothing is relevant unless it gives first place to the material. But what man thinks is relevant and what God says is relevant may be two different things. "Labor not," said Jesus, "for the meat which perisheth" (John 6:27).

By this time the crowd was getting intrigued. "Lord," they said, "give us this bread." And Jesus answered, "I am the bread of life; he who comes to me shall not hunger, and he who believes in me shall never thirst" (John 6:35, RSV).

Then followed a remarkable dialogue. Some of the crowd became offended because Jesus insisted that men must believe in Him, that they must eat His flesh and drink His blood, in order to have eternal life. A crisis occurred, and John records that "many of his disciples drew back and no longer went about with him" (John 6:66, RSV). As long as He offered bread for their stomachs, they would follow Him. But when He talked about eternal life, they began to murmur, "Why, this fellow isn't relevant," and they went looking for a more popular prophet.

Then Jesus turned to the twelve remaining disciples

and said to them almost wistfully, "Will you also go away?" Notice carefully what Peter answered, "Lord, to whom shall we go? You have the words of eternal life" (John 6:67, 68 RSV).

"To whom *shall* we go?" That's the question I'd like to ask those who say that Christ is out of date. If we are going to abandon Christ, if we are going to leave and forget Him, to whom *shall* we go? Who's got the answer? Who *is* relevant?

To whom shall we go with our great burning *social problems?* To whom shall we go for the answer to war? To whom shall we go for the answer to broken homes? To whom shall we go for the answer to hatred and race prejudice? Abraham Lincoln once said, "I have often been driven to my knees by the realization that I had no other place to go."

Shall we go to the scientist? Science has made fabulous strides toward better living. But science has also created monstrous weapons that could destroy civilization.

Shall we go to the educator? We should all be thankful for what our schools have done. But if we educate men's minds without changing their souls, we are just turning out smart devils.

Shall we go to the politician? Certainly we need better laws. But all the laws in the world can't make men love instead of hate.

No, Jesus Christ is not unconcerned about social problems and material needs. Jesus never said, "Man shall not live by bread." He did say, "Man shall not live by bread *alone*" (Matt. 4:4). He cared about the hungry crowds, and He fed them. But He refused to run on a platform of making bread. He knew that the root of our material problems is a moral malady, and the root of our moral disease is a spiritual sickness.

Dr. W. B. Harvey, former professor of political science at the University of Western Ontario, has said, "In mechanical advance the essence of the problem is

105

invention; the use of the invention is almost automatic. But in moral, economic, or political advance the problem is to get people to act on a new or higher plane."

And that is precisely why Jesus two thousand years ago said, "(You) must be born again" (John 3:7). New technology without new men simply creates new and more fearsome problems. And that is where the relevance and the absolute imperative of spiritual conversion comes in.

Some people believe that Christians ought first to deal with the political and social emergencies of the world and then deal with unseen things. They say that the world is like a man in the water drowning. The first thing to do is not to preach the gospel to save his soul but to pull him out of the water to save his life.

That sounds plausible, but it is not really true in our deepest dilemmas. The emergencies in our world have not been caused merely in the physical realm but by the evil in the souls of men. It takes just a simple physical effort to pull a drowning man out of the water. But to pull society out of the whirlpool is not a simple physical effort. It is a difficult task which involves changing men's hearts. Certainly, a spiritual change will not solve all our problems. But it will provide a foundation from which we can become part of the answer.

To whom shall we go for the answer to our *personal problems?* Dr. Louis Evans was visiting White Sands, New Mexico, at the missile proving grounds. A scientist was describing to him the amazingly intricate calculations which were made to send a rocket to the moon. Dr. Evans said that his brain was reeling, when suddenly the scientist turned to him and said, "Dr. Evans, you are a man of God, aren't you? Then for God's sake, help me. My wife is leaving me tomorrow morning!" He was a professional success and a personal failure.

For all of our vaunted progress we have not eradicated the deep longings of the human heart. What Jesus said two thousand years ago is still relevant! Jesus is still the Bread of Life, and men still need that bread.

Psychologists say that men want significance, security, love. Philosophers believe that men are concerned about guilt, death, and the meaninglessness of our existence. Jesus says that these deep drives can be satisfied when we find life—genuine life, authentic life, new life, eternal life, God's life.

You see, the Bible teaches that we have been cut off from God's life because of sin. "The wages of sin is death" (Rom. 6:23). We have lost contact with God and have rebelled against Him. We have broken His laws and have forgotten Him. We have tried to shut God out and run our own lives, with disastrous results. That is why we are afraid of death, why we're cursed by guilt, why our lives seem to have no meaning. We are like leaves plucked from a tree and severed from the source of life.

The Bible teaches that God has provided the answer to this problem of sin. Jesus said, "I am the bread of life" (John 6:35). At the Last Supper He took a piece of bread and broke it and said, "This is my body . . . broken for you" (1 Cor. 11:24). At the Cross the flesh of Jesus Christ, the Son of God, was broken. He took our death to make a great exchange and to give us His life as bread to satisfy the hunger of our souls. The quest for significance, for love, for forgiveness, for meaning, for eternal life, can be satisfied only in Him. Jesus said, "He who believes on me shall not hunger" (cf. John 6:35). He also said, "This is the work of God, that you believe on him who sent me" (cf. John 6:29).

Jesus Christ is relevant not only in the emptiness of life but in its fullness. He brings comfort to the sick and purpose to the well, healing for the broken home and new joy for the whole one, abundant life for the beginning of the road and eternal life at the end.

You may say that Jesus Christ is not right. You may

deny His claims to be the Son of God and the Savior, but you cannot say He isn't relevant. The problems Jesus talks about are the deep problems of modern life. To whom shall we go to change our world and to change our lives?

"Will you also go away?" said Jesus.

And Peter answered, "To whom shall we go?"

Exactly. If we turn our back upon Christ, who else can meet our deepest need?

A man who has been a missionary for many years in China, Ham Hamilton, a man who has seen the adequacy of Christ to meet human need, has written these lines:

> Here is a broken heart,
> Shot through with throbbing pain;
> Only the healing touch of Christ
> Can make it whole again.
>
> Here is a broken life,
> Ruined by shame and sin;
> Only the burning love of Christ
> Can make it pure within.
>
> Here is a broken home,
> Bitter and undone;
> Only the alchemy of Christ
> Can fuse it into one.
>
> Here is a broken world,
> Shattered by war and hate;
> Only the Christ triumphant
> A new world can create.*

---

*From *Afraid? Of What?* by Rev. E. H. Hamilton, D.D.

# 13

# Bring Us Together

ON INAUGURATION MORNING January 1969, a very excited and proud thirteen-year-old girl sat in the stands at Washington, D.C. There were many distinguished guests who came to the inauguration. But Vicki Cole and her family were the especially invited guests of the president of the United States.

In late October, Mr. Nixon was on a whistle-stop tour of northwestern Ohio. Vicki, whose father is a Methodist minister, had made a poster, but at the last minute she couldn't find it. So in desperation she picked up another sign off the street and waved it frantically.

Vicki never guessed that someone had paid special attention to the sign she was holding. And that someone was Mr. Nixon himself. Vicki's sign carried a plea, "Bring us together," and that caught Mr. Nixon's eye and stayed in his mind. Later he told this story and said that the sign carried by Vicki had inspired the theme of his inauguration, "Forward together."

It seems to me that no theme speaks more to the hearts of people at this time. The plea on Vicki Cole's sign is the plea of the nation and of the world, "Bring us together."

The walls that divide men are growing faster than we can tear them down. Isn't it ironic that in the twentieth century we have learned to swim like fish in submarines, to fly like birds in aircraft, but we haven't learned yet to walk like brothers on the earth? Men have walked and worked in the peaceful and still atmosphere of the moon while at the same time the very fabric of American life was ripped by dissension and bigotry and suspicion. As the president said, "We have found ourselves rich in goods, but ragged in spirit; reaching with magnificent precision for the moon, but falling into raucous discord here on earth."

America today is in danger of becoming a series of growing gaps—the racial gap, black against white; the generation gap, young against old; the poverty gap, haves against have nots; the domestic gap, husband against wife; the ideological gap, conservative against liberal; the industry gap, labor against management.

The division is not only an American problem. Every nation seems to have its own split. In Canada it's French-speaking versus English-speaking. In Northern Ireland it's Catholic versus Protestant. In England it's immigrant versus native Englishman. In East Africa it's African versus Indian. In Southeast Asia it's mountain tribes versus lowlanders. Never was there a time when we so much needed someone to bring us together!

But the danger is that we will asume that there is a superficial way of bringing people together—that with goodwill and political savvy and modern communications there is a simple solution. But there is no simple solution. There is a deep root to divisions among us which no one, however sincere he is, however intelligent he is, can solve. I am convinced that we will never bring people together until we realize that this is more than a political problem or a psychological problem or a communications problem. It is "a crisis of the spirit."

There was a time when men were as one; yet the Scripture says that "Cain rose up against . . . his brother, and slew him" (Gen. 4:8). There was no language barrier, no racial issue, but there was violence. There was a time when men were as one; yet the Scripture says that "God saw that the wickedness of man was great in the earth, and that every imagination of the thoughts of his heart was only evil continually" (Gen. 6:5). No language barrier, no racial issue—yet there was worldwide immorality. There was a time when men were as one; yet men said, "Let us build . . . a city, and a tower, whose top may reach unto heaven . . . And the Lord said, Behold, the people is one . . . now nothing will be restrained from them. . . . Let us go down, and there confound their language" (Gen. 11:4, 6, 7).

What made Cain kill his brother? What made men think "only evil continually"? What made men aspire to build a city reaching to heaven? Whatever it was,

111

God found it necessary to restrain them by confounding their language and scattering them.

We like to boast of our sophisticated nuclear space age. But we're not so very different from the people described in the first eleven chapters of Genesis. We still have our violence and our evil and our overweening pride. Man still tries to find unity in alliances which leave God out. Take away languages, remove racial issues, and you will not eliminate man's divisions. The problem runs deeper.

On one occasion Prince Philip was asked in a television interview about racial problems. This is what he said, "Racialism is not just a matter of color. . . . There is a lot of tribalism in us still. A few hundred years ago there was only one Book that was read—the Bible. . . . In the days of God, so to speak, everyone was seen as equal in the sight of God. This made for antiracialism. But take away God, and we have to revert to tribalism again." Now Prince Philip was right. Only God can bring men together.

We have failed to herd men together by laws and by treaties and by regimentation because our efforts have only been on the horizontal level. But if we would only expose individuals and groups to the upward pull of the Spirit of God, then they would come together.

As I have traveled and preached around the world, I have seen the literal fulfillment of the promise of Jesus, "If I be lifted up . . . (I) will draw all men unto me" (John 12:32). Men and women of all races and all cultures and all ages have come to Christ, and in coming to Him they have come to each other.

From the very beginning Jesus Christ has been tearing down the walls that divide. One of the greatest divisions of all time was that between Jew and Gentile. And yet Christ made a bridge over this gap. In Ephesians 2:15 the Apostle Paul wrote, "Having abolished in his flesh the enmity . . . for to make in himself of twain one new man, so making peace." "Having abolished . . . the enmity"—how man hungers for an end to hostility—". . . to make in himself . . . one new man." How man hungers for oneness!—"So making peace." How men hunger for peace! But how?

Paul had found a sense of oneness in Christ. The whole second chapter of Ephesians is Paul's witness to the Christ who can make men one. Over and over again he uses the word "together." Christ has "raised us . . . together," Christ has brought us together.

In ancient Jerusalem in the temple there was an outer court of the Gentiles, the only part to which foreigners were admitted. Three feet above that was the Sacred Enclosure, to which all Gentiles were forbidden under penalty of death. At the very center was the Most Holy Place, closed off by a curtain, where only the high priest could enter once a year on the Day of Atonement to make atonement for the sins of the people. "But," says Paul, writing now to Gentiles, "now in Christ Jesus you who once were far off have been brought near in the blood of Christ. For he is our peace, who has made us both one, and has broken down the dividing wall of hostility . . . that he . . . might reconcile us both to God in one body through the cross, thereby bringing the hostility to an end" (Eph. 2:13–16, RSV).

According to Matthew's Gospel, when Jesus died, the veil of the temple that divided off the Most Holy Place was torn in two (27:51). This was the sign that the way was now opened for sinful men to have fellowship with God and that in Christ all distinctions between races and sexes and classes became irrelevant.

Jesus Christ didn't end the enmity by settling all the questions and removing all the distinctions. He bridged the differences. He transcended them by giving to believers a new loyalty, a new status, that made other distinctions trivial and meaningless. The woman is still woman; the man is still man. The illiterate is still uneducated, and the professor is still learned. The Negro is still dark, and the white man, light. But now all who believe in Christ are one in Christ. No wonder that eventually this exploded slavery. And no wonder that this can overcome the prejudice and the snobbery of the world today!

I heard about a new Christian in India who saw two factions of his tribe fighting with iron-tipped poles. He ran between them and took the blows on his own head, and the blood began to flow and to stain his clothes. They stopped fighting. Some of them ran to get a doctor; others took him into their home. From that moment a reconciliation took place—a reconciliation through blood. This man said, "If a few drops of blood of a sinful man can reconcile a village, how much more can the blood of the Son of God reconcile the whole world!"

Now, what is it that divides us from God? What is it that divides us from our brother? It's our sinful, selfish pride. That's why Christ had to die on a Cross. That's why His death and resurrection are God's answer, God's way to bring men together. It's only as the love of God conquers us at the Cross that we can stop trying to conquer each other.

Lesslie Newbigin tells a story which shows the supernatural power of the love of Christ to bring men together. In South India he met a group of Christians who were led by a curious man who indicated to his fellow Christians when to stand up and to sit down with a stainless steel baton.

It seems that this Indian evangelist was in Burma preaching the gospel when World War II broke out. The Japanese arrested him, took away all his belongings, and threw him into a corner. A Japanese officer looked at the table where his belongings were and picked up his Bible. He recognized it was a Bible though he didn't know a word of this man's language, and he held up his hand and made the sign of the cross.

Now the evangelist didn't know a word of Japanese,

but he realized the Japanese officer was asking if he were a Christian; so he nodded, "Yes."

The Japanese officer came and stood in front of him, stretched out his arms in the form of a cross, cut his bonds, gave to him his officer's staff, and set him free. And this was the baton Bishop Newbigin saw him wielding.

William Barclay comments on this story, "Here were two men who knew not a word of each other's language, two men from nations which were at war, two men between whom there stretched a gulf which, humanly speaking, was beyond bridging—and Christ bridged that gulf. Jesus Christ reached out across the divisions and brought two men together."

The only way men can come together is when we find at the Cross the power to fulfill Jesus' words, "Blessed are the peacemakers, for they shall be called the sons of God" (Matt. 5:9, RSV).

Now, how can we become peacemakers?

First, get right with God. The Scripture says, "God was in Christ, reconciling the world unto himself. . . . Be ye reconciled to God" (2 Cor. 5:19, 20). God crossed the sin gap. He bore the sins of mankind on that Cross.

Second, get right with your fellow-men. Forgive "as God for Christ's sake has forgiven you" (Eph. 4:32, Phillips). Remember that Jesus said, "If you do not forgive men their trespasses, neither will your Father forgive your trespasses" (Matt. 6:15, RSV). It may be that your employer has hurt you, or your employee or your husband or your parents or your friends or your neighbor. Forgive them! It may be you have hurt somebody else. Go and ask his forgiveness and put things right.

Third, look for ways to love those who are on the other side of the fence from your group. Jesus said, "Love your enemies and pray for those who persecute you" (Matt. 5:44, RSV). Wouldn't it be wonderful if for the next 100 days every Christian in America would look for some way to "overcome evil with good" (Rom. 12:21)?

You say, "But I'm only one person." Yes, you are. You can't do everything. But you can do something. Remember that a thirteen-year-old girl in Ohio picked up a sign and influenced the next president of the United States.

Every four years the inauguration of a new president solemnly marks the transfer of political power in the United States. But today can be your Inauguration Day, the start of a new era, if you will transfer the power and the control of your will to Jesus Christ as Lord and ask God to make your life a signpost for the power of the living Christ to "Bring us together."

# 14

# This Thing Called Love

IN THE PREFACE to his autobiography Bertrand Russell once wrote that three passions governed his life—a longing for love, a hunger for knowledge, and a deep pity for the suffering of mankind.

When Lord Russell wrote about a longing for love, he struck a responsive chord, because it seems that everybody today is talking about love. There is a popular slogan, "Make love, not war." And there is a song entitled "The Word," taken directly from chapter one of John's Gospel. It says, "Have you heard the word is love?"

Some time ago in Pittsburgh I saw a psychedelic poster. It had a series of one-word questions and answers:

| | |
|---|---|
| Who? | You! |
| What? | Love! |
| When? | Anytime! |
| Where? | Anywhere! |
| How? | Anyhow! |
| Why? | Because you are you! |

Now as Christians we agree that love is the greatest thing in the world. Probably the most famous verse in the Bible is John 3:16. In twenty-five words it sums up the message of the Bible, "For God so loved the world, that he gave his only begotten Son, that whosoever believeth in him should not perish, but have everlasting life." The core of the Bible is the love of God. Jesus said that the Ten Commandments are summed up in love to God and love to our neighbor (Matt. 22:37—40). He also said, "By this shall all men know that ye are my disciples, if ye have love one to another" (John 13:35). Paul said, "Love never fails" (cf. 1 Cor. 13:8).

Yes, as Christians we agree that love is important. But we also believe that there are some very important questions that we have to ask before we understand love. We have to ask, Why love? What is love? And how can we learn to love?

First of all, we have to ask, *Why should we bother to love at all?*

Recently I stood in the intensive care unit of a hospital watching a team of nurses and doctors working desperately to save a man's life. He was a derelict, a drunk, who had been picked up off the street. And I thought to myself, "Why do we have hospitals with tender, loving care trying to save lives of people we might think of as being derelicts? Why do we have this kind of concern? Why do we need love to be human?"

We can only draw one of two conclusions. We can say that man is just an accident, that there is no God, that man is related downward to the animals and the machines. We can say that love is an accident of chemistry, the by-product of chance, and a fanciful illusion.

On the other hand we can say that love is not an accident, not a mistake, because man is related upward to God. And that is why the burden we have to love and to communicate is real. Man is made in the image of God (Gen. 1:27), and God is love (1 John 4:8). You see, that is the importance of the fantastic, staggering truth that we read in John 3:16 (RSV), "God so loved the world that he gave his only Son."

The message of the Bible is this: God is; He is the God who is really there. God is love—not a cold, impersonal, far-off, uncaring deity, but a God who has a personal concern for us. And, "God so loved the world that he gave his only Son."

The psychedelic poster said love *is* because you are *you*. But there is more than that. Love exists because God is God, because He is the God of the Bible. And you are you—you are made to be loved because God made you.

When Jesus was on earth, on one occasion He prayed, "Father, I have loved men with the love I had with

You before the world was" (cf. John 15:9). You see, before there were ever any human beings, before this world was here, there was love. Why? Because God is love, and in the Trinity the Father loved the Son and the Son loved the Father and the Holy Spirit.

Why bother to love? Because God is God. Otherwise, the love game is the biggest put-on in all history.

But there is another question we have to ask, *What is love?* Love is a word we throw about so casually, but do we know what love is about? Whether it's a teenage crush or an extra-marital affair, a missionary abandoning the comforts of home to live in the hardness of some far-off brush country or a promiscuous sexual fling, we call it love.

So, what is love? According to this tremendous verse, God had demonstrated what love is in one solitary Life. "God so loved the world that he gave his only Son." You want to know what love is? God says, "Look at My Son. See what I have done in giving My Son for you."

Some months ago there was a prize-winning film named *Warrendale*. It was about a Canadian hospital for disturbed children. The therapy in this hospital was based on the belief that a lack of physical affection contributed to the children's illness. So they put a lot of emphasis on physical touching. Some of the child patients were even held forcibly and hugged while they cried and struggled—until finally they relaxed and learned to receive the touch of love.

Jesus Christ was God's touch of love—God's love touching our need in our real world. Jesus was God's love touching flesh in a virgin's womb and lying in a manger. Jesus was God's love touching the things of work as He handled the saw and the plane in the carpenter's shop. Jesus was God's love touching the sores of the leper and the sightless eyes of the blind. He was God's love touching the children as He held them. He was God's love touching the bread, breaking it at the Last Supper and saying, "This is my body . . . broken for you" (1 Cor. 11:24). He was God's love touching our sins as He laid His hands on the rough wood of a cross to be pierced by the nails, bearing the shame and scars of our sin. "Here is love," says the Bible, "not that we loved God, but that he loved us, and gave his Son to be the atonement for our sins" (cf. 1 John 4:10).

It is so important that we understand that God's love was not just words or not just an emotion. It was love in action. It involved the will of God. "God so loved . . . that he gave his . . . Son." God saw the need of sinners who were perishing and acted to meet that need.

You see, the love of God didn't mean that He ignored our sin or overlooked our sin or condoned our sin. Sometimes I have heard people say, "Oh, God is love, so everything is going to be all right. God won't judge." Oh, no! That is not the God of the Bible. God is love, the Bible says, so He gave His Son in order that we could have a way out of our terrible predicament. The Bible says the human race is perishing, separated from God, under a death sentence because of our sins. And God came in His love because we were under condemnation so that we would not have to be condemned. But if we refuse His love, we condemn ourselves to an eternal lostness (John 3:18).

The third question about love is, *How do we get the capacity to love?* Psychiatrists today say that the ability to love is a prime mark of emotional maturity. And it is certainly the crowning mark of the Christian. But to "love your neighbor as yourself," as Jesus commanded (Matt. 22:39, RSV)—that's quite a challenge. Notice exactly what He said. We are to love our neighbor as ourselves.

Even if I don't like myself, I still love myself in the sense I want the best for myself. I may not like myself when I make a mistake. I may not like myself if I have a bad habit. But still I want the best for myself. Jesus

121

says that is how God loved us. Even though He didn't like our sins, He willed the best for us and He gave His Son that we could be saved. And that is how we are to love our neighbor. Even though we don't like everything about him, we are still to want the best for him.

There's a popular song that goes, "What the world needs now is love." Right. That's true. We know it's true. But how in the world do we get the power to love? If we're going to give love, then first of all we have to receive the love of God and to have the life of God and the power of God within us. And that is why John 3:16 (RSV) is so significant, "God so loved the world that he gave his only Son, that whoever believes in him should not perish but have eternal life."

You see, here's a wonderful thing. When I *believe* in Jesus Christ, when I turn my sins and my selfishness over to Him for His cleansing, then the Holy Spirit brings the very life of God to *live* within me; and His *love* begins to operate in my soul. Believe! Live! Love! That's the order. As Paul said, "(Christ) loved me and gave himself for me," and, "Christ . . . lives in me" (Gal. 2:20, RSV).

God knows we don't have the power to love, and that is why He has done two things: First, He sent His Son to the Cross to die for our sins; and second, when we put our trust in Christ, He sends His Spirit into our hearts to work out this love in us.

If we are to learn to love with genuine love, we must take these three steps: First, admit honestly we don't have the power to love; second, put our trust in the God who loved and died for us on that Cross; and third, ask God by His Spirit to lead us to some specific act of love for some person we find very difficult to love. Then we are to act as if we loved him. And when we have taken these steps, we will find God beginning to make a tremendous difference in our lives.

Some time ago a university student told me how the love of Christ had begun to transform his life. He comes from a broken home. His mother has remarried, and he and his stepfather hated each other. In their family there was every conceivable problem—alcohol, drugs, psychological problems.

Four years ago somebody invited him to a ranch in Colorado where everyone was centered around the person of Jesus Christ. After a period of spiritual struggle he was able to turn his life over to Jesus Christ. And he said, "Do you know something? Nobody ever told me this would happen. But when I got back home, I found that hard lump of hate for my stepfather beginning to dissolve. Instead I began to understand him, to have an affection for him, and even to love him. This was the result of learning that Jesus Christ really loved me."

I'd like to amend that poster I saw in Pittsburgh this way:

| | |
|---|---|
| Who? | You! |
| What? | God's love for you. |
| When? | Right now! |
| Where? | Wherever you are this instant. |
| How? | Open your life by faith to Him. |
| Why? | Because God is God; and God so loved you, that He gave His only begotten Son, that if you would believe in Him you would not perish, but have everlasting life. |